JEMEZ. N.M.

ISLETA N.M.

AN FELIPPE N.M.

INDIAN CHURCH
ZIA. N.M.

PALA MISSION
PALA. CALIF.

E.A. BURBANK.

1940

BURBANK AMONG THE INDIANS

CHIEF GERONIMO.
APACHE.
1898.

BURBANK AMONG THE INDIANS

by

E. A. BURBANK

AS TOLD BY ERNEST ROYCE

EDITED BY FRANK J. TAYLOR

ILLUSTRATED BY
E. A. BURBANK

THE CAXTON PRINTERS, LTD.
CALDWELL, IDAHO
1 9 4 6

First printing December, 1944
Second printing February, 1946

Printed, lithographed, and bound in the United States of America by
The CAXTON PRINTERS, Ltd.
Caldwell, Idaho
62207

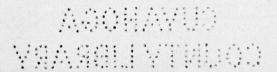

DEDICATED TO MY UNCLE
EDWARD E. AYER
AND THE
NORTH AMERICAN INDIAN

"MANY BRUSHES"—INDIAN PAINTER

Without the least disparagement to the art of Brush, Farny, Remington, and others, and not forgetting the powerful sculptures of Proctor, Kemeys, Boyle, Dallin and MacNeil, it is entirely within bounds to say that no one has at all rivaled Burbank as an historical painter of Indians. He has taken up, barely in time—for all the Indianness of the First Americans is disappearing wonderfully fast—one of the least hackneyed, most picturesque and most important fields possible to American art. And he has proved, very emphatically, his entire competence to dominate it.

Incidentally, one reason why Mr. Burbank can paint Indians lies back of his fingers, and was not learned in the art schools. He can not only see but understand. They are to him not merely line and color, but human character. More ignorant people, who fancy that aborigines are not quite men and women, might be enlightened—if anything can enlighten them—by talk with this unassuming painter. His ethnologic horizon is not scientifically exhaustive; but he has got far enough to understand the fact of human nature—and this is much deeper in wisdom than many who pass for scientists, and write monographs of large words, ever made. One could make a very interesting story of Burbank's experiences and impressions in this career of painting Indians; a superficial acquaintance, in one way,

but enabled by unspoiled eyes to arrive at the foundations
of comprehension.

Born in Harvard, Illinois, Mr. Burbank began his art
training in the old Academy of Design, Chicago, in 1874. He
studied in Munich from 1886 to 1892. He is a nephew of
Edward E. Ayer of Chicago, first president of the Field
Columbian Museum, a trustee of the Newberry Library,
and a collector and owner of the finest private library of
Indian Americana in this country.

Admirably grounded in character portraiture by his long
and highly successful studies of Negro types, he was turned
westward by Mr. Ayer and began on Indians in Oklahoma,
thence working northwest into the Sioux, Cheyenne and
Nez Perce country. Later he traveled much among the
Southwestern Apaches, Navajos and Pueblo stocks—particularly the Hopis, Zunis and Queres—and again among
the Southern Cheyennes, the Arapahoes, Osages, Ogallala
Sioux, and so on. He has painted most of the more famous
chiefs—Geronimo, the last Apache genius, many times—and
a great store of typical men, women and children.

Mr. Burbank has in general selected very characteristic
types; and his portraits are done with rigorous exactness.
He nothing extenuates, nor sets down aught in malice. He
neither idealizes nor blinks. From our personal point of
view, his pictures are harsh—not "retouched" as we demand
our artists to flatter us, but uncompromising as a photograph made in strong sunlight. Popularly, this may give a
mistaken impression; for many will forget that one chief
reason why an Indian is so much more furrowed and ugly
than we are is because he has no retoucher to make him
pretty. But scientifically this insistence upon the lines in
which life indexes character, is very important.

Mr. Burbank preserves not only the facial type with
extraordinary fidelity and smypathy; his portraits are as
well a graphic and accurate record of the characteristic
costumes, tribal and ceremonial. This is an uncommon

service, not only to the future but to the present. The vast majority of our painters and illustrators seem to have neither sense nor conscience about this matter. They are as apt to dress a Pueblo in a Pawnee warrior's dress, or a Kiowa in ancient Aztec costume, as anything else; and still more certain to confound the faces. It would not be quite so ridiculous to portray Quakers in cowboy garb, or Yankees with the physiognomy of Italians. But they do it, right along, and never seem to feel that they are either stupid or mendacious.

It is a peculiar merit of Mr. Burbank's art and conscience that he sees these vital differentiations and regards them. He is by odds the most successful thus far of all who have attempted Indian portraiture. His work has historic truth and value for which we seek in vain, from Catlin down to date, for a parallel. As Lungren is doing the best and truest work yet done on the southwestern arid landscapes and atmospheres, so Burbank is easily master of Indian faces.

CHARLES F. LUMMIS, in *The Land of Sunshine.*

CONTENTS

ILLUSTRATIONS

14   ILLUSTRATIONS

BURBANK AMONG THE INDIANS

GERONIMO, THE APACHE

When an Indian accords you his friendship—or his hatred—he gives all without reserve. So it was with old Geronimo,* the Apache, the first Indian on my canvas. Before I learned whether I was "good medicine" or "bad" with Geronimo, I experienced some uneasy moments.

This wily, daring old Apache had won for himself a fearsome reputation throughout the country, when my uncle, Edward E. Ayer, president of the Field Museum in Chicago, commissioned me to go to Fort Sill in the old Indian Territory, and paint Geronimo's portrait.

For many years the Apaches had roamed like Arabs over the desert of southern Arizona and northern Mexico, defying the efforts of both the American and Mexican armies to subjugate them. The Apaches were fighters, feared by other Indian tribes and by white settlers. Under Geronimo's command, they had waged a fierce guerrilla warfare,

---

* The name Geronimo was given to him by the Mexicans. His Apache name was Goi-Yacht Ley which means "to yawn."

leading first the American troops, then those of
Mexico, a merry chase across mountains and deserts.
But at last Geronimo's band was captured and he
was held as prisoner of war at Fort Sill. It was there
I journeyed in search of him on what was to be the
first of twenty years of hunting the real Americans
for my canvas.

Having heard of Geronimo only through the
screaming newspaper headlines which exploited his
daring raids and cruel massacres, I was prepared to
meet a thoroughly bloodthirsty savage. I gave
thanks that I did not have to encounter this crafty
Apache at large, but instead could sketch him behind
prison bars.

Imagine my great surprise, upon arriving at Fort
Sill, to find that Geronimo was not in prison at all,
but was allowed his freedom. He lived in a house the
government had built for him—a one-story affair
built around a patio. A small Indian boy helped me
to locate it. He said Geronimo was taking a nap.
After hesitating a bit, I decided to rap and take a
chance on incurring the old warrior's wrath. There
was no answer. Then the Indian boy came running
back.

"I forgot," he said. "He is out hunting horses."

I sat down upon the steps and waited. Presently
an elderly Indian came riding up on a horse and
dismounted. He was short, but well built and muscu-
lar. His keen, shrewd face was deeply furrowed
with strong lines. His small black eyes were watery,
but in them there burned a fierce light. It was a

wonderful study—that face, so gnarled and furrowed. I studied it as he came over to me.

"How do you do, Chief Geronimo?" I greeted him.
He shook hands with me gravely.

"How!" he said.

I learned later that it was fortunate for me that
I had addressed him as "Chief." The soldiers at Fort
Sill had nicknamed him "Gerry"—a name that an-
noyed him greatly.

Through the Indian boy, Geronimo asked me my
reason for being there.

"To see the Indians and the country," I told him.
Geronimo asked where I came from.

"Chicago," I said.

I offered him a cigarette and lighted one myself.
We sat there and smoked for awhile without saying
anything. All this time Geronimo was peering at
my face. He knew I had some further object in being
there. Finally he asked me to tell him about Chicago.

I described the tall buildings, the lake, and elevated
railroads. For perhaps ten minutes he allowed me
to talk about the things in Chicago which I thought
would interest him. Finally he rose and said, "Come."

I followed him into the house. He delved into an
old trunk and brought forth a photograph of himself.
As he handed it to me he said, "One dollar."

I gave him the dollar. It occurred to me that this
was the time to make my proposal for painting his
portrait.

"I am an artist," I said. "I also came to Fort Sill to
paint a picture of Big Chief Geronimo."

The old Apache looked at me questioningly.

"Are you a chief?" he asked.

I gathered that he meant "Are you any good?" I assured him that I was.

"All right," he said. "When will you come?"

I told him I would be back next day, but upon my return to the fort I learned I would have to secure the permission of Captain H. L. Scott, the commanding officer. He happened to be in Texas looking for cattle for the Indians. But he was expected home soon. I waited.

Upon his return Captain Scott not only granted permission to paint the portrait of Geronimo, but he invited me to attend a powwow with the Indians that evening. At this council there were present the chiefs of several of the tribes on the reservation, notably the Kiowas, the Apaches, and the Comanches. An interpreter accompanied each chief except Geronimo, who did no talking.

Captain Scott's talk was entirely about the cattle he had been trying to get for the Indians. The chiefs hung on every word he said. How different this gathering from a meeting of white men! After each speech the speaker who followed would wait a full minute before saying anything to be sure the other man had finished his remarks.

During the powwow Chief Looking Glass arose and said, "Captain Scott, I have never before shaken hands with a white man, but I would like to shake hands with you now."

The incident showed how much Captain—later

Chief Naiche, Apache, 1899.

E-wa, daughter of Geronimo, Apache, 1898.

E-ney, an Apache Belle of Geronimo's Band, 1898.

Chief Tal-klai, Apache, 1898.

Brigadier General—Scott was loved by the Indians. To them he had become the Great White Father.

Next morning I was on hand bright and early at Geronimo's house to start work on his portrait. I found him ready and eager to pose. But just after I had outlined the sketch in pencil he held up his hand.

"Stop!" he commanded. Calling the little Apache girl who was playing near by, he asked her to interpret a message to me.

"This man wants to know how much you are going to pay him," she said.

"I was stumped for a minute, but finally said, "Ask him how much he wants."

I learned then that Geronimo was something of a Scotsman.

"You get much money for that picture," he said. "Maybe five dollars. I want half."

I told her to tell Geronimo that if he would sit for two pictures he could have all of the five dollars. He agreed to do this.

I never had a finer sitter than Geronimo, although sometimes he became very nervous while posing. I would give him a few minutes' rest until he quieted down. Invariably upon hearing a horse or footsteps, he would rush to the door and see who was coming. He seemed to have a haunting fear of being pursued, even though he was at the time a prisoner.

As we worked day after day, my idea of Geronimo, the Apache, changed. I became so attracted to the old Indian that eventually I painted seven portraits of him.

For that first portrait he sat on the bed and I on a box. There was not even a chair in his house at that time. Geronimo inveigled me into buying him one, which I did at the cost of five dollars. He was good at that game. One day while I was painting, a man came along with a sack of grain for sale. The old Apache worked me to buy that for him also.

I tried to get Geronimo's real character into the portrait I was making. I painted every wrinkle in his face and even a mole on his cheek. Being fearful that he might object, I would not let him see the picture at first. However, one day when I left my easel to get some water, I returned to find Geronimo intently studying the portrait. I waited on pins and needles for his verdict. Suddenly he turned, laughed, and slapped me on the back.

"You heap big medicine man," he said. "You heap big chief. You heap savvy."

I remembered that remark and turned it on him one hot day when the temperature stood at 110 degrees in the shade and Geronimo complained that it was too hot for him to sit any longer.

Filling his mouth with water, he squirted it into the air, calling out, "Rain. Rain."

"Look here," I said, "didn't you tell me once that I was a medicine man?"

He admitted that he had.

"Medicine man must be obeyed," I said. "You sit."

"All right," said Geronimo. "I will."

Geronimo's money-making schemes were many and varied. Once he was permitted to make a trip to Omaha by train. At each station where the train stopped he got off, mingled with the people on the platform, let them know who he was, and then sold the buttons off his coat for twenty-five cents apiece. Between stations he sewed new buttons back on again. He also sold his hat for five dollars whenever he could find a buyer. He had a reserve supply of hats and buttons in his suitcase.

The soldiers at Fort Sill, knowing Geronimo, were kind to the old Apache and taught him to write his name. After that he charged a dollar for his autograph.

One day Geronimo asked me if I had a gun. I told him I had a small .22 caliber rifle and he asked me to bring it over the next time I came to his house. I did so. Geronimo looked at the rifle, took a piece of paper about the size of a quarter, and pinned it to a tree several yards distant.

Then he proposed that we fire at the piece of paper in turn. Every time he hit the target I would give him ten dollars and every time I hit the target he was to give me ten dollars. I looked at his small, bleary eyes and seriously considered taking him up. But he seemed overly anxious, so I said, "No, we'll shoot for fun."

It was lucky for me that I did that, for he hit the paper every shot, and once hit the pin that held it. I never made a hit. In spite of his watery eyes, Geronimo's sight was remarkable for a man of seventy.

He was a great gambler and was ready to bet on

any event that offered him a chance of adding to his bank account. Incidentally, at the time of his death he left more than ten thousand dollars in the bank.

One day Geronimo invited me to go with him to a sports meet of the soldiers, Comanches, and Kiowas. He said he would be the only Apache there, with the exception of some boys who were going over to play ball. He wanted me to stand back of him when he played cards, claiming that I brought him good luck.

The popular game was monte. Geronimo was always in the game up to his neck. It was fun to watch him handle the cards. He was as expert as the best of them. At times he would get excited and yell at the top of his voice. The betting was always on the turn of a card. And when Geronimo was dealing he would cover the money each time. No one could bluff him.

Once the bets piled up to something like one hundred dollars on a turn of the card, while Geronimo was dealing. He reached into his pocket, but found no more money there. He looked up at me and I thought he was going to strike me for a loan. But instead, he delved into another pocket and pulled out a reserve roll of bills as big as his hand. When the card was turned, Geronimo won. He gave a war whoop that could have been heard for a mile as he hauled in the stakes.

As we were leaving for home, a white man approached Geronimo and proposed that they race horses. He offered to bet ten dollars that his horse could beat Geronimo's. We walked over to look at the white man's horse, and Geronimo decided to take the bet.

Ordinarily Geronimo, in spite of his age, rode his own pony. But this time he thought he was too heavy. He looked around for an Apache boy to ride his horse. The boy he wanted was playing baseball, and was at bat when Geronimo went after him. The Indian boy swung at the ball, narrowly missing the old chief, hit the ball into the outfield, and then started running the bases. Geronimo tore after him, all the way around the diamond, and chased the boy across the home plate before he caught him.

That horse race demonstrated the old Apache's sporting instincts. He was ready to bet on anything. They marked off the distance, placed the stakes in a handkerchief at the end of the course where the winner could grab it, and the horses were off. It was a close race, which Geronimo's horse won. The old Indian went home as happy as a small boy after the circus.

Once while I was painting him Geronimo asked me what I did with my old clothes. I told him I gave them away.

"Send them to me," he said.

I agreed to do so, but on second thought told him that we had better find out if they would fit him. He stood about five feet four inches, but had very broad shoulders. I took off my coat for him to try on. It was much too small for him and he nearly ripped it to pieces trying to get it on. So I told him that there was no object in sending my old clothes to him if they would not fit him. This seemed to satisfy him.

A few days later I left Fort Sill and did not return for a year. Upon my return I set out to call upon Geronimo. On my way to his house I met him coming along on horseback. As soon as he recognized me he pointed his finger at me angrily.

"You lie!" he said.

We had become close friends and the accusation came like a bolt out of the blue. I could think of nothing that I had told the old Indian that he could have construed as a lie. Since Geronimo's pidgin English was insufficient to make clear to me what was wrong, I grabbed his horse by the bit and led him all the way back to his home to find an interpreter. Geronimo claimed I had promised to send him my old clothes, but I had failed to do so. I reminded him that he had tried on my coat and that it was too small for him and that we had agreed there was no use sending my old clothes to him. This seemed to stir his recollection. He dismounted, apologized, and shook hands.

Though Geronimo was willing to pose for me for a price, he objected strenuously when a famous eastern museum asked the officers at Fort Sill to make a plaster cast of his hand.

"Toda, toda," he repeated. "Toda" is Apache for "no."

Finally the officers asked me to help persuade him. I explained that the cast could do no harm to him, but the answer was still "toda." Seeing the wet plaster lying there on the table, I seized his hand and pressed it in, making a fine cast, which has been much studied by palmists.

In the rest periods Geronimo would lie on his back on the bed and sing Apache songs to me. He had a deep, rich voice and these songs, sung in the Apache dialect, were of great beauty. One of them, translated, ran as follows:

> O, ha le
> O, ha le
> Through the air
> I fly upon a cloud
> Toward the sky, far, far, far,
> O, ha le
> O, ha le
> There to find the holy place
> Ah, now the change comes o'er me!
> O, ha le
> O, ha le

One day Geronimo initiated me into the art of massaging as it is practiced by the Apaches. Following his directions, I bared my back and lay flat on my face on the bed. Doubling up both fists he rubbed and massaged my back like a woman kneading bread. It was strenuous treatment, but the after-effect was a grand and glorious feeling. I think the old Apache did this for ulterior motives, because after he had shown me how it should be done, he frequently would lie face down and ask me to massage his back, which I did.

When I worked out at Geronimo's house I always brought my lunch. I usually brought extra food so that I could offer some to him. He seemed to enjoy white men's food, but for some reason he was cautious and sniffed each morsel carefully before he would take a bite.

One day he invited me to take dinner with him. The meal, while clean and good, was served very crudely. It consisted of meat, bread, and coffee, cooked by his wife and served on a plain board which she placed on the ground before us. There were no knives, forks, or spoons. We had to eat with our fingers. Two years later Geronimo again invited me to dinner. What a difference between the two meals! This time I sat at the table with Geronimo, his wife, and daughter. The table was covered with a linen cloth. There were knives, forks, and spoons. They served a splendid dinner complete with a dessert. This is typical of the readiness with which the Apaches adapted themselves to the white man's way of living.

Geronimo's wife, a very small woman, was in poor health. So the old war chief did all the housework, washing the dishes and sweeping the floor. He was an immaculate housekeeper.

One day I carelessly tracked some mud into the house. Geronimo got the broom and swept it out, giving me a look which plainly said, "Don't do that again." Thereafter I was one white man who was very careful not to track any mud into an Indian's house.

Geronimo had a little daughter about six years old, named E-wa, of whom he was very fond. No man

Chief Santos, Apache, 1898.

E.A.BURBANK.
SAN·CARLOS.
ARIZ.

Siem-o-nad-o, Apache, 1898.

Chief Many-Horses, 1898.

E. A. Burbank's Studio at Ganado, Arizona.

could be kinder to a child than Geronimo was to little
E-wa. In spite of his parsimonious attitude towards
outsiders, he was so indulgent with E-wa he would
give her anything she wanted, and nothing in the
trading post was too good for her.

Indians are notably fond of children. And nothing
pleases them more than to have a white person show
their children attention and kindness. An Indian
himself will be as kind to a white child as to one of
his own race.

When I was at Fort Sill, a little boy living in Chicago came to Fort Sill to visit his brother who was
a lieutenant stationed there. One day the lad was
missing, but the lieutenant did not worry, as he had
heard the child had gone with some Kiowa Indians,
and so knew he was all right. It was amusing to hear
the boy talk when he came back. He said he had had
the time of his life, had slept in the tepee with the
Indians, and had eaten with them. They had made
bows and arrows for him, had given him a pony to
ride while he was with them, and taught him Indian
words and songs.

One of Geronimo's hobbies was writing letters to
his friends, especially the Apaches in San Carlos,
Arizona. Several times he asked me to write these
letters for him. They were fine epistles, well com-
posed, and almost always he asked them to send him
a certain medicine which the San Carlos Apaches
prepared.

Geronimo was a medicine man among his people.
Invariably his letters ended with this line: "If you

are in need, let me know and I will send you money."

The old warrior never left his house without putting out a saucer of milk for his cat, whose whiskers he had kept closely clipped. Why he used the scissors on tabby I never did learn.

Geronimo's small nephew was invariably about the house. One day Geronimo excused himself for a short time, saying he had to go to the store. He told his nephew to entertain me. The little boy gravely invited me to sit on the floor. Then he sat opposite me about ten feet away and rolled a stone to me. We spent the hour until Geronimo returned rolling the stone back and forth between us.

For one of my portraits of Geronimo I wanted him to pose as a savage warrior on the warpath. I would hate to have him on my trail looking as he did that day with his war paint on, holding a large six-shooter in his hand.

Geronimo had not painted his face for the warpath for a long time. The correct Apache way was to paint a white stripe about a half inch wide from ear to ear across his cheeks and nose. Instead of painting one stripe Geronimo painted two. He would never have noticed the error had not his wife laughed at him. When she explained the cause of her merriment he hastily changed it to one stripe.

One day he came into my quarters at Fort Sill in a most peculiar mood. He told me no one could kill him, nor me either, if he willed it so. Then he bared himself to the waist. I was dumfounded to see the number of bullet holes in his body. I knew he had been in many battles and had been fired on dozens of times, but I had never heard of anyone living with at least fifty bullet wounds on his body. Geronimo had that many scars.

Some of these bullet holes were large enough to hold small pebbles that Geronimo picked up and placed in them. Putting a pebble in a bullet wound he would make a noise like a gun, then take the pebble out and throw it on the ground. Jokingly I told him he was probably so far away that the bullets didn't penetrate him, but that if he had been nearer they probably would have killed him.

"No, no," he shouted. "Bullets cannot kill me!"

As I knew Geronimo, I find it hard to picture him as the leader of a band of ravaging savages. To me he was a kind old man. To be sure, he had his peculiarities, and his outlook on life was not the same as a white man's, but he was certainly not as cruel as he had been pictured. Geronimo and the Apaches had been much misunderstood. Geronimo was not the chief but the medicine man of the Chiricahua Apaches. He usurped the leadership of the tribe under the stress of unusual circumstances.

While I was at Fort Sill an editor of a magazine offered me a considerable sum of money if I would get the story of Geronimo's life. I talked with Geronimo about this and he, with his usual Scotch acumen, agreed to tell me his life story in return for half of the proceeds. So, accompanied by a good interpreter, I went to Geronimo's house one Sunday morning to get the story. He lay on his bed with his hands folded behind him and began to talk.

"The first thing I remember," Geronimo said, "was noticing what a large number of Indians there were."

He said that when he was a young man the Apaches, after a long council, decided to be friendly with the white men. To celebrate this momentous decision they gathered together with their families and were having a great feast. While they were in the midst of this feast, a company of Mexicans rode up on horseback. The Mexicans were soldiers, he said, and they brought with them much whiskey which they gave free to the Apaches, but refrained from drinking themselves. When the Apaches had become helplessly intoxicated, the Mexicans shot into them, killing forty-six Indians and wounding many more.

As Geronimo came to this point in his story he became intensely excited. He rose from his bed, his dark face almost white with anger as he shook his fist in my face, fairly hissing, as he declared, "After that I killed every white man I saw."

The Indian boy who was acting as interpreter became greatly excited too.

"He is telling you the truth," he said, "for my father tells me the same story."

Geronimo said that this was the first time he had ever told anyone that part of his story. He begged me to go and return later. He was too excited to continue his story that day. Later on he told me that he himself had missed the massacre because he was in town on an errand, but that on his return he had found his father, his mother, his wife and children all dead, lying in a pool of blood on the ground.

If this story is true, and I have no reason to question it, it was not surprising that Geronimo waged war on the whites with bitterness and skill both in Mexico and in the United States.

By nature the Apache is industrious, honest, and loyal to his friends. At Fort Sill the Apache homes and gardens were the neatest on the reservation. Fences that surrounded their yards were well kept up. Every man took his turn at riding the fence. None of the other tribes were as devoted to duty as the Apache.

The third time I returned to Fort Sill I met Geronimo riding horseback through the woods. On his horse he had with him both his daughter E-wa and his little nephew. He assumed I had returned to paint more pictures of him. He pointed his finger at me.

"You make heap money painting my picture," he said. "You pay me so much."

He held up both hands twice and one hand once, indicating that I must pay him twenty-five dollars to paint him again.

"You are wrong," I said. "I did not come to paint your picture this time. There are other chiefs I want to paint."

On this trip I persuaded Chiefs Naiche, Mangus, Chato, Chewawa, Loco, and Geronimo's little daughter, E-wa, to pose for me. All of the chiefs wore their scout costumes, which were very picturesque and colorful.

Naiche was the head chief of that branch of the Apaches. I had been anxious to meet him, but had not encountered him. One day I was sketching a wickiup when I noticed a tall, fine-looking Indian watching me. I spoke to him and asked him if he knew where I could find Naiche. He laughed.

"I am Naiche," he said.

Naiche had the reputation of being the finest Indian artist of that period. He painted his pictures on deer skin in color. His subjects were flowers, deer, other wild animals, turkey, and various objects of nature, as he saw them. He also carved canes from wood and painted them in different colors. I asked Naiche how much he would charge for a painting on a deer skin. His price was three dollars and fifty cents. I discovered that the deer skin had cost him three dollars. So I raised his price to ten dollars when I bought one of his pictures.

Naiche told me that in one of the fights between the American soldiers and the Apaches he had received a bullet which passed completely through his chest. He fell and the soldiers cheered, thinking they had killed him, but before they could reach him he recovered enough so that he could mount his horse and escape.

After I had painted the Apache chiefs at Fort Sill, I journeyed to San Carlos, Arizona, to make the pictures of Chief Santos, Chief Chil-chu-ana, and Chief

Bi-lish. I also persuaded several women to pose for me.

While one of these women was posing for me one day, the army officer in charge of the reservation dropped in. After the woman left, he told me this story about her.

This Indian girl was married and had one child, he said. There were still some Indians hiding away in the mountains. They had never been rounded up by the soldiers. One of these renegades wanted a wife and set about to capture one. He mounted his pony, rode two hundred miles, and arrived at San Carlos Reservation at night. Scouting around, he found this girl alone with her mother and her baby. He killed the mother, tied the baby and girl on his horse and took them to his camp in the mountains.

He watched her closely for many days. She acted as though she were satisfied with her fate. Eventually he became careless, sometimes leaving her for half a day at a time while he was hunting. Finally he left for a trip that would take two days. As soon as he was out of sight she snatched up her baby, caught a horse, and was soon galloping down the mountainside. She covered the two hundred miles to San Carlos with hardly a stop, arriving there safely.

The army officers contended that the Apaches were the best scouts in the world. They told me several stories to prove their claim.

Once when the soldiers sought to capture a band of Indians who had committed several crimes, several friendly Apaches were delegated to help bring these

renegades in. For some distance the trail was plain.
Then it faded out at a spring where cattle herds came
from all directions to drink. Here the trail was hope-
lessly lost to the ordinary person, but not to the
Apaches, although it proved quite a problem even
to them. They dismounted and on their hands and
knees studied the ground. The officer in charge
finally asked them what they had found. Pointing
to a small twig on the ground, one of them said:

"That has been pushed aside by a moccasin."

After a powwow they separated into two parties,
to come together at a point twenty miles distant,
where they found their quarry and captured them.

Another story is that of the Apache Kid. He was a
boy distinguished for his great industry. Another
Indian killed his father. The Apache Kid went to the
officers and asked them why they did not capture and
punish the slayer. The officers replied that they
could not find him.

The young Apache asked permission to go after
his father's slayer himself. In a joking mood they
told him to go ahead. Two days later, while the officers were eating their supper, the Apache Kid
appeared.

"I have killed the man who killed my father and
here is the proof," he said.

With that, he reached into a sack and brought out
an Indian's head which he threw on the table.

They placed him under arrest. Later on, with two
other Indians he was started off to prison at Yuma.
The Apache Kid was shackled by one leg to the seat

of the wagon. Coming to a steep hill, the driver asked the two deputies and the two other Indians to get out and walk to lighten the load. The day was hot and the deputies grew careless. The two Indians afoot crept up behind the two deputies and knocked them insensible. Securing the keys, they overcame the driver, released the Apache Kid and were on their way. The other Indians were soon recaptured, but not the Apache Kid.

One day while I was talking to an old Indian I mentioned the Apache Kid. He said that the Kid was still alive, though an old man, and that he knew where he lived. He had changed his name and called himself Is-niz-zi.

At the San Carlos Reservation I painted the portrait of Tal-kla, a courteous, kind-hearted Apache chief; and also Chil-chu-ana, a big fat jolly chief who, with his red blanket draped over his shoulders, would have passed well as a monk.

Chil-chu-ana and Geronimo were boys together. He was delighted when I told him I had painted Geronimo. Chil-chu-ana was distinguished by being the last of his tribe to surrender to the United States Army.

As I painted Indian chiefs, my portraits were reproduced in magazines and newspapers, and I collected these into a scrapbook which soon became for me a pass into any Indian home or gathering place. It was astonishing to see how interested each Indian was in these pictures of other Indians. They would sit and examine the pictures by the hour and criticize the detail of the costumes. I soon learned to be very careful of details so that the Indians would know that my pictures were faithful reproductions.

The Indian girls were especially interested in the costumes worn by the other girls. They would point to each one and ask about the other girl and how she made her costume. Some they would criticize, saying they did not like the clothes.

Often the Indians would come to me and ask if they could borrow the scrapbook. Many times I have gone into Indian quarters to find the room full of natives turning the leaves of the scrapbook and looking at the pictures. They would do this so often that I had to paste and repaste five different scrapbooks. Geronimo kept my scrapbook for several days, delighted with the pictures I had painted of some of his boyhood friends. Some of them he had not seen for many years.

My last parting with Geronimo was quite sad. I think the old man realized that we would not meet again. As I bade him good-by for the last time he told the interpreter to say to me:

"I like Burbank better than any white man I have ever known. He has never lied to me and has always been kind to me and my family."

Geronimo's death occurred at Lawton, Oklahoma. His daughter E-wa had died a few years before. Riding home on horseback through a storm, in his seventies, he got wet and chilled and contracted pneumonia. While still conscious, he called for his horse.

He asked to have him bridled and saddled and the reins placed in his hands.

When the old warrior died, the horse was shot so that Geronimo, the Apache, would have a mount to ride to the Happy Hunting Grounds.

THE NAVAJOS—AMERICA'S BEDOUINS

It is an odd trick of fate that the Navajos, who of all Indians have developed the keenest commercial sense, should be the least affected by the white man's ways. They roam the great open spaces south of Grand Canyon and live like Bedouins, following their flocks of sheep and goats across the desert just as their forebears did.

The Navajos are first cousins of the Apaches. A Navajo and Apache can understand each other if both speak slowly. But where the Apaches were warriors, the Navajos became artizans and traders, skilled as rug weavers, silversmiths, and at barter.

Although the Navajos and the Apaches spring from the same racial stock, it was the custom of the former to make raids upon the surrounding tribes, notably the Hopi, the Shoshones, the Zuni, and the Pueblos, and to carry off their women. Thus the Navajos assimilated the blood of several Indian nations, and there is consequently no true type among them. Some are short and stout like the Pueblos.

Others have the tall and slender build of the Plains Indians.

These American Bedouins do not call themselves Navajos, which is a Spanish term, but "Dene" which means "the people." The Navajos feel quite superior to the surrounding Indian tribes. They conduct themselves with lofty independence, and when the occasion demands it a Navajo can look straight through another Indian or white man without seeing him, as if the latter were too inferior to be noticed.

To me no picture of a Navajo scene is complete without that of J. L. Hubbell, the generous, hearty Indian trader who operated the trading post at Ganado, Arizona; the man whom the Navajos called "the old Mexican," and who—as Stewart Edward White said in a description in one of his books—"is afraid of neither God, man, nor the devil."

I first heard of Mr. Hubbell when I arrived at Gallup, New Mexico, looking for Navajos to paint. Clint Cotton, the old Santa Fe telegraph operator who ran the trading post in Gallup, took me in hand.

"Go down to Ganado and see Hubbell," he said. "When you get there give this to him and tell him to shave himself."

He handed me a safety razor.

Arriving at Ganado, I found Hubbell looking like a wild man with a beard hanging to his belt. He welcomed me heartily and invited me to occupy a room in his house. But he refused to shave.

"How much is it going to cost to live here?" I asked.

"It will not cost you anything," he replied.

"Then I won't stay," I said. "I will have to find quarters where I can pay for them."

The old Indian trader looked genuinely hurt.

"I have been here for thirty years," he said, "and I have never yet charged anybody anything for either food or lodging. Are you going to make me break my rule now?"

I stayed, but eased my conscience by presenting him with pictures, and by copying rug designs for him.

Mr. Hubbell was a friend of every Indian in the Navajo nation. He was born and reared in the Navajo country. His mother was a Spanish woman. His father an American. He used to be sheriff of Apache County. Once when he was arresting a horse thief, the bad man turned and drew a bead on him. Many-Horses, chief of the Navajos, took the situation in at a glance and shot the thief, saving Hubbell's life. That was the beginning of one of the finest friendships I ever encountered between a white man and an Indian.

Mr. Hubbell turned over his office to me for a studio. Because of his influence upon the Indians, I had no trouble in getting the Navajos to pose for me. My first sitter was his good friend Many-Horses. He posed wearing his colorful Navajo costume of head chief. The old Indian liked the portrait so much that he asked if he might pose for another picture. I told him to come back on the following day.

Imagine my consternation when Many-Horses appeared again in his Navajo costume, but in addition he was wearing a tall stovepipe hat which had been presented to him by a tourist. I urged him to take the hat off, explaining that no one would want a picture of an Indian in such a garb. Many-Horses was terribly disappointed. He left the studio completely crushed. In a short time he was back. This time he had the plug hat decorated with eagle feathers. I decided that such perseverance should be rewarded. So I painted him, plug hat and all. Much to my surprise, Mr. Hubbell was delighted with the portrait, and bought it. He had a cut made of the picture and used it on his stationery.

Many-Horses and Mr. Hubbell used to joke with each other about the Happy Hunting Ground.

"If you die before I do," the trader told the old chief, "I will put a rope around your neck and drag you to the top of the hill. I will put the largest stone I can find on top of you so that you can never go to the Happy Hunting Ground."

Many-Horses would laugh. "You die first, and I do that to you," he would say.

While I was at the trading post Many-Horses did die. I helped Mr. Hubbell bury him on top of the hill. True to his promise, the Indian trader put the largest stone he could find at the head of the Indian's grave, crying like a baby while he was doing so. Later on, both he and Mrs. Hubbell were buried beside Many-Horses.

The Hubbell trading post was not only the general

store, but it was likewise the bank and everything else for the Navajos. Mr. Hubbell ran a pawn shop where the Indians would bring their valuables and pawn them when they needed money. Sometimes articles were left for years. When the Indians returned with the money, Mr. Hubbell would return the articles deposited. He never charged interest. The tags in the pawn shop were records of each Navajo's financial state over a long period of years.

The trader made money, but he seldom received it from the Indians. They almost always paid for food or clothing in baskets, blankets, and jewelry. Many times I have seen Navajo women come in and say that they needed flour, sugar, and coffee, but had no money.

"Give this woman what she wants," Mr. Hubbell invariably called to a clerk.

Several times Mr. Hubbell said to me, "I am going to quit being so softhearted." But he never did.

One day a party of men came on horseback. Each man was armed with a six-shooter.

"What will you charge us for meals and lodging and food for our horses?" the leader asked.

"Nothing," said Hubbell. "Put your horses in the stable."

The men came in.

"You'll have to take those guns off," said Mr. Hubbell. "Put them on the table. What do you think this is, the wild and woolly West?"

They did as he told them. Next morning before they left they picked up the guns from the table. The party continued to Gallup, New Mexico, where they robbed a gambling house, staging one of the biggest holdups in that part of the country!

All who came were welcome to the Indian trader's hospitality. One day a boy showed up and asked if he could stay overnight, explaining that he had no money.

"Sure you can stay," said Mr. Hubbell. "Where are you going?"

The boy was going to Chin-Lee, thirty-five miles away, where he had been promised a job. He was going to walk across the desert.

"You are not going to do anything of the kind," said the Indian trader.

He provided not only a horse, but an Indian to accompany the boy to Chin-Lee.

One of the Indian trader's good friends was Man-u-let-o, a head chief of the Navajos. He once was a powerful man among the Navajos. While Man-u-let-o was in Gallup, New Mexico, the noted sculptor, Herman McNeil, made a life-size statue of him. Clint Cotton, who ran the Gallup trading post, bought the statue and placed it above the main entrance to his store.

Shortly thereafter a road show came to town. One of the attractions was a ventriloquist. He came into the trading post and asked Cotton to teach him a few Navajo words. Then, taking a position near the door, he threw his voice so that the words seemed to come from the mouth of the statue.

The Indians gathered there were so alarmed that

they fell all over each other getting out of the trading post. They refused to come near the store, even though Cotton explained to them over and over again that it was just a trick. He lost that group of customers for good.

Once while he was in Gallup, Man-u-let-o attended a rousing revival meeting. He became so interested in temperance that he took the pledge to abstain from liquor. He returned to Ganado wearing his blue ribbon and vowing he would never touch a drop of whiskey again. This was the old chief's one weakness, and Mr. Hubbell encouraged him in his good intentions.

A few days later Man-u-let-o invited Mr. Hubbell to come to a temperance meeting the Navajos would hold. They were going to combine it with a ceremonial dance. Man-u-let-o said he was going to give a lecture on temperance.

The old chief gave an eloquent talk on the evils of drink to the group of Indians gathered in a corral. There was one Indian in the crowd who was already under the influence of liquor. Acting on drunken impulse, this Indian made his way up to the speaker and produced a bottle of whiskey. He invited Man-u-let-o to have a drink. The old chief resisted for a while, but eventually the fumes were too much for him. He accepted the bottle and took a long drink, continuing his lecture with the half empty bottle in hand.

As he waxed more eloquent, he would pause occasionally to refresh himself. Finally the words became all mixed up and Man-u-let-o wandered over to the side of the corral where he went sound asleep. The rest of the Indians went on with the dance without paying any attention to him. The fallen temperance lecturer lay there on the ground all night, contracting a chill which turned to pneumonia. Shortly Man-u-let-o died.

Never have I seen a man more understanding of Indian psychology than Mr. Hubbell. No problem of any Indian was too large or too small to merit his wholehearted, sympathetic attention.

Once, while I was staying with him, his branch trading post at Cornfields, Arizona, was struck by lightning. No Navajo will subscribe to the theory that lightning never strikes twice in the same place. They refused to trade at the store struck by lightning and would not touch the goods that had been in it. Mr. Hubbell solved their boycott by loading his stock in a big wagon one evening and hauling it off before the Indians' eyes. Driving out into the desert, he rearranged the load under cover of darkness, and drove back next day with his "new stock." The Navajos were satisfied and business was carried on as usual.

One day a Navajo boy herding a flock of sheep unintentionally let them stray on a white man's land. The man angrily ordered the boy to get them off quickly. The young shepherd was doing so as fast as he could, but the man impatiently drew a gun and shot one of the sheep.

With a show of spirit characteristic of his race,

the Indian boy shot one of the white man's cows. The man shot another sheep, and the boy shot another cow. After which the white man fired at the boy, barely missing him. The youngster then took aim at the man and killed him with a single shot.

This young Navajo was tried for murder and sentenced to Yuma Prison for life. Believing that the boy had received a raw deal, Mr. Hubbell turned heaven and earth in his behalf and finally succeeded in having him pardoned.

The Navajos raise some corn for food, but their wealth is principally in their flocks of sheep, goats, and ponies. They are among the wealthiest Indian tribes in the country.

Che Dodge, a very wealthy Navajo who made his money dealing in sheep, is typical. Because his name was Dodge, he purchased a Dodge car, and had a white man drive it for him. He lived in a fine residence on the Navajo reservation, and sent his children to an eastern college to be educated.

Wherever the Navajo builds his campfire is home. Usually he builds two campfires—one for the animals to gather around, and the other for his family. The Navajo's house is a round log hut with one door in it always facing east. This is known as a hogan. It resembles a huge beehive. In the center of the roof is a hole a yard or so across, opening to the stars above. Below this hole he builds his fire so that the heat will warm all parts of the hogan, but the smoke will escape through the hole. In the summertime while he is on the move, the hogan is usually made

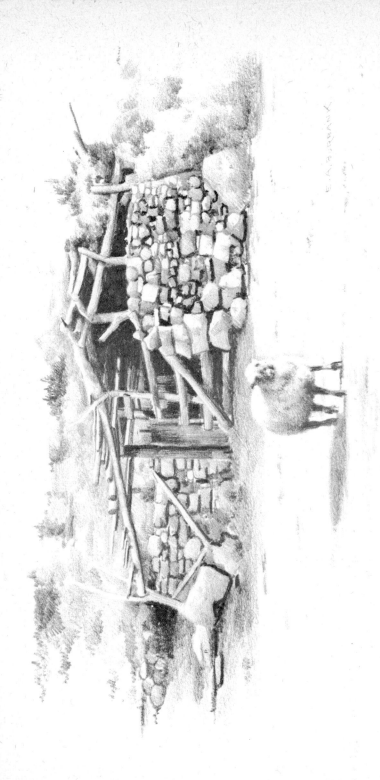

Navajo Sheep Corral.

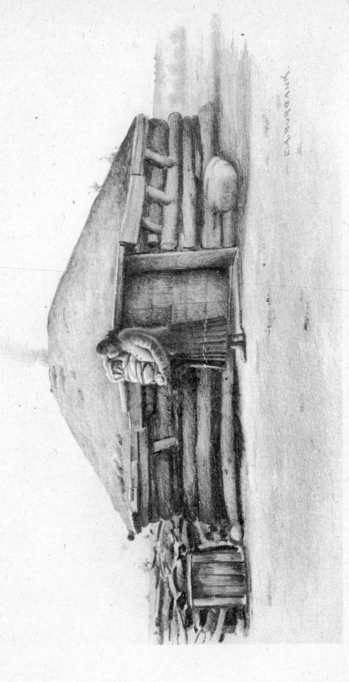

Navajo Indian Mother, Her Child, and Hogan.

of brush plastered with mud. While they are on the move these nomads of the Painted Desert build their campfires in the shelter of a ravine or a cliff.

According to legends passed on by word of mouth from one generation to another, the Navajos first secured sheep and goats from the early Spanish settlers in Mexico, probably in the sixteenth century. Prior to that time the tribes lived by hunting and by raiding their agricultural neighbors, the Pueblos.

Among the Navajos there is a curious division of property. The hogan, the sheep, and the goats belong to the women. The horse saddles and jewelry belong to the men. If a Navajo woman tires of her husband, she can divorce him by merely placing his saddle outside the door of the hogan. This, I might add, is seldom done. The Navajo family ties are close. They are particularly devoted to their children, who learn to ride ponies before they can walk, so that they can follow the flocks along with their elders. The children help their parents in herding sheep, and sometimes they do all the work themselves. They are good herders.   46–17657

The little girls dress exactly like their mothers, and comb their hair the same way. I have seen them weaving blankets, and have seen the little Indian girl in the hogan cooking meals for her younger brothers and sisters when their parents were away.

The Navajo children, especially the little girls, are more superstitious about posing for their portraits than the children of other tribes. One little girl, for instance, refused to sit for me because she had had a bad dream about posing for me. The boys are shy of strangers.

At one time a Navajo chief had the right to as many wives as he could purchase and support. But this custom has disappeared, although wives are still obtained by purchase, the transaction being carried on entirely between the prospective groom and his chosen mother-in-law. The girl has nothing to say about it.

After he is married, a Navajo will not look at his mother-in-law for fear of going blind. I have seen a Navajo start into a store, then beat a hasty retreat because his mother-in-law was doing some shopping.

One old Navajo chief living in a remote part of the extensive reservation was discovered with several wives. The Indian agent told him to pick out the one he wanted to keep and send the others back to their mothers. The old Indian listened to the instructions carefully. After some thought he spoke for the first time.

"You tell 'em," he said.

The Navajos have a dance which they call the Ya-be-chey. It lasts all night and is an interesting ceremony. Unlike most Indians, the Navajos sing and dance at the same time. They are quite willing to hold their dances in public and visitors are almost always invited. Usually these dances are held in a corral.

The Navajos are particularly devoted to their medicine men who give no medicine whatsoever. It is strange that a people so intelligent in other ways should believe so devoutly in the power of incantations to cure their illnesses.

The medicine men place all of the patients in a tribe in a single hogan. The "doctor" who undertakes the cure sings and yells at the top of his voice, dances and jumps about, and waves his hands toward the hole in the top of the hut. The Navajo idea is that illness is caused by the presence of devils in the body. The "Doctor" is supposed to drive the devils out of the body and up through the hole in the top of the hut.

So great is the influence of the Navajo "doctors" that they are frequently called in by the surrounding Indian tribes. The Hopi women especially have great faith in Navajo medicine men for their children. I have seen as many as twelve Hopi mothers sitting on the floor each holding a sick child while a huge Navajo shouted, yelled, and waved for the devils to leave the children and go out through the hole in the roof.

One day I was painting a Navajo woman and her child. This mother had been to school and was fairly well educated. I noticed that the little girl's body was covered with sores. Earlier that morning I had also observed that she had called in a Navajo "doctor" to hold his incantations, trying to heal the child. My sympathies for the youngster overcame me and I could not resist speaking to the mother.

"You are an educated woman," I said. "You know that Navajo medicine men cannot cure your child. Why don't you take her to the government doctor?"

My words were all that she needed to swing the balance between her superstitions and her better judgment. She took my advice and the youngster was soon cured.

Often these "sings," as the Navajo medicine men's ceremony is called, are abetted by sand pictures as a medium of curing illness. The relatives of the sick person gather around while the medicine man, using different colored sands, makes a picture on the floor. These sand pictures are supposed to have a mysterious power for good.

If for any reason the sand pictures and the "sing" fail to free the Navajos of the microbes, and the ill person dies, his body and his effects are burned with the hogan, and no healthy Navajo would think of entering a house in which anyone had died.

Another strong superstition among the Navajos is that having to do with the coyote. They will not kill the coyote, though they know it kills their sheep. For they believe the coyote takes their soul to the next world.

A surprising custom among the Navajos is that of having the women do all of the butchering. They are very skillful butchers, as was demonstrated one day when a Navajo woman whose picture I had painted came to me on a rainy day and asked if she might butcher a sheep in my studio. This seemed an unusual request, but inasmuch as she promised not to do any damage, I consented. She performed the operation without getting a single drop of blood on the floor.

The Navajos are excellent cooks. Their favorite way of cooking meat is to broil it on sticks held over an open fire. They also cook a sheep's head without removing the brains from the skull. After the cooking they break open the skull and eat out the brains.

The Navajos are most devoted shepherds for the thousands of sheep which they herd across the desert with the aid of sheep dogs, in search of grass. The Navajo boys are trained to do this work as soon as they can ride. Every boy has an empty bag tied to his saddle. Any stray lambs which are deserted by their mothers are carried to the hogan in this bag, to be raised by hand.

All Navajos are industrious and as soon as they pause in their never-ending trek across the desert, the women resume work on their rugs and the men take up their silver work. The Navajo jewelry is artistic and is made entirely by the men from Mexican dollars which they melt down and pour into moulds. From this they make buttons for their clothes, bracelets, and hammered silver belts.

However accomplished the Navajo men might be as silversmiths, it is the Navajo women who have made the nation famed the world over with their blankets and rugs.

Prior to the coming of the white man these blankets were made in only three colors: white, gray, and black. The designs were worked out by mixing the wool of white and black sheep. When the American traders arrived in the Navajo country they brought with them yarns which gave the Navajos a wider range of colors. Reds and greens blended well in the Navajo designs.

The first red that the Navajos used came from a finely woven cloth traded to the Indians by a party of English travelers and traders. This was known as Bietta cloth. The Navajos patiently unravelled this cloth and added these yarns to their blankets. These blankets are now very rare and even a small one will bring a good price.

Later the traders who bought the rugs insisted upon the use of purple and yellow which brought about a clash of colors. Then the commercial spirit of the Navajos worked to the disadvantage of their artistry and soon the rugs and blankets lost much of their original beauty of design. I have often seen the traders instructing squaws how to make blankets, telling them to work in more colors, to use pinks and purples and to leave less "bare space."

The beauty of a genuine Navajo blanket is its simplicity of design and harmony of color. Like most children, the Indians are close copyists and their eagerness to give the traders what they want accounts for the loss of artistry in weaving as well as color blending.

The finest Navajo blanket I ever saw was one at Mr. Hubbell's, measuring twenty-five feet square. It was an inch thick and had been sold to a New York club for several hundred dollars.

The Navajos are supposed to have learned the art of weaving from the neighboring Hopis. Tradition has it that the Hopis taught the Navajos to weave in exchange for assurance that the Navajos would cease their raids on the Hopi villages. Curiously, among the Hopis the men are the weavers, whereas among the Navajos the women do all the rug making.

In olden times the Navajos and Hopis were bitter enemies and waged constant warfare. The Navajos were the aggressors. The Hopis, being a peace-loving people, lived largely by peaceful pursuits. Many and bitter were the wars between these two peoples.

The Navajos and the Hopis are still whole-hearted rivals in a more peaceful way. They are keen traders, but the Navajos invariably have the advantage. Whenever groups from the two nations get together they indulge in horse racing and other sports, with many side bets on the results. The Navajos invariably win the horse racing because they breed and raise better horses. However, the Hopis make it up in foot races, since they are able to outrun any Navajo or any other Indian.

One of the outstanding memories of my happy days among the Navajos was the Christmas I was invited by Mr. and Mrs. Charles Bierkemper, missionaries at Ganado, to help them in a feast they were giving for the Navajos at their little church. They had a Christmas tree laden with presents for the Indians, and after a fine address by the missionary, I was appointed Santa Claus to help pass out the food and presents among the Indians.

The guests had not been limited in the number of dogs they could bring. Consequently each family had from one to a dozen dogs there. After all the men, women, and children had been fed, I told them that Santa Claus Many-Brushes was going to see that all the dogs had a Christmas dinner. I fed the dogs with the remains of the feast. This pleased the Navajos so much that they burst out in a cry of "Yachte, yachte." This means "good," and established my standing permanently among these American Bedouins.

THE FASCINATING PUEBLOS

Of all the one hundred and twenty-eight Indian tribes among whom I have lived and worked, the most fascinating were those of the Pueblo group—the Hopi, Zuni, Acoma, Laguna, Zia, San Iltel Fonso, Namba, Jamez, Isleta, Santo Domingo, and Tewa tribes. Among some of them I was welcomed; among others I painted at the risk of my life.

To this day it astonishes me to think of a people as intelligent and skillful as the Pueblos living shackled by superstition and witchcraft. The Pueblos have been more or less under the white man's domination since 1540, when the Spanish explorers first found them. Yet four centuries of contact with the white man find the Pueblos still living primitively in isolated tenements constructed of clay in the characteristic architecture which has so greatly influenced our own throughout the southwestern states.

Long before the white men came, these town-dwelling natives of the desert had developed a considerable civilization of their own. Surrounding

them on all sides were ruins of cliff dwellings pointing to an even greater Indian culture. The Pueblos
spoke four distinct languages. They are related more
closely to the Indians of central Mexico than those
that live near them, and it is believed that their culture was an offshoot of the ancient Mayan civilization which preceded that of the Aztecs. All the
Pueblos were remarkable Indians in that they had
learned how to till the soil, raise their own food, and
store it against droughts. They had also become
skillful artizans at pottery, basket making, and
weaving.

They usually built their homes on mesas. Often
their pueblos were reached only by ladders which
could be drawn up when enemies threatened them.
Because of this aloofness, I found portrait painting
among the different Pueblo tribes an exciting adven-
ture. Certain tribes, notably the Hopi, made me welcome. Others, such as the Zunis and Santo Domingos,
bade me be gone. Invariably I ran headlong against
traditions and superstitions which made the life of
an artist difficult.

The Zunis believed that anyone who made a line
of another person was a witch. As soon as I arrived
among this isolated people they nicknamed me
"Witch Man."

Inadvertently I chose as one of my first subjects an
old woman who had recently been accused of witch-
ery. This old squaw lived near a Zuni family, one of
whose children had died suddenly. The Zuni medicine men concluded that she had bewitched the child

and caused its death. After a powwow they seized her one night, rushed her to a church, and hanged her to a rafter.

Other Zunis, more sensible, arrived in time to cut her down before she died. She was revived and lived to have her portrait painted by the "Witch Man," an act which did not improve the reputation of either of us. In fact, shortly after she sat for me I was earnestly advised by friendly Zunis to leave their village, which I did.

It was eight years before I returned to their pueblo. When I came back they recognized me immediately, but were more friendly. I asked them if they still considered me a witch.

"No," said one of their chief medicine men, "we do not believe in witches any more. We have learned better."

After that I was permitted to paint portraits among them without serious objection.

Not so with the Santo Domingos.

My first contact with these aloof Indians was at another pueblo where two Santo Domingos were visiting. Wishing to meet some of the tribe, I went over to them and extended my hand to one of them. Since he could not avoid it, he shook hands, but he was anything but enthusiastic about doing so. I told them I wanted to come to their village to paint the portraits of some of their chiefs, and had arranged with the government Indian agent to visit them. The agent had provided me with a letter to the "governor," as the head man in any Pueblo tribe is known.

In spite of these preliminary arrangements I learned when I set out for the village of Santo Domingo that the Indians had put two guards on the trail to head me off before I entered their village. So I took a roundabout trail and reached the village by the back door, so to speak, before they were aware of it.

At the first house I asked where I could find the governor. I thought at first that the big six-foot Indian who came to the door was going to attack me. But instead he rushed past me, motioning me to follow him. He led me to a dim council chamber where I found several Indians holding a powwow. The upshot of their discussion was that the interpreter advised me to leave at once. I pled with them to let me return on the following day and show them my portfolio. After some hesitation they agreed.

The next day I found the same group assembled. They immediately became very much interested in my paintings and examined them carefully. I thought that I had overcome their hostility. Imagine my astonishment when, after a brief discussion, the interpreter turned to me and said, "We have seen your pictures, now get out."

I told the interpreter I had heard a good deal about the Santo Domingo Indians, and asked him if he would care to hear what was told me. He replied, "Yes. Tell us."

"I was told you treated the school teacher, who was a woman, so badly that she left. This morning I looked in the schoolhouse and discovered that you are using it as a stable for horses.

"The government wanted to build you a good flume, costing twenty-five thousand dollars, to take the place of the old one which leaked and caused you a lot of trouble. But you would not allow it to be built.

"The government, in order to have a good well dug for you, had to have soldiers with Winchester rifles to keep you Indians off until the well was dug. It was a good well. But as soon as the well was finished, you Indians killed a burro and threw it into the well to spoil the water.

"A lady took some photographs of your village. You took her camera and broke it, then gave it to her and ordered her away.

"Is all this that I have told you true?" I asked the interpreter.

"Yes," he answered.

"But why do you do such things?" I asked.

He did not answer.

"Do you want me to tell you what I think about it?"

"Yes," he replied again.

"I think you Indians do not use good judgment."

But by no amount of pleading could I change their decision. The most I could wheedle out of them was permission to paint portraits of any Santo Domingo who happened to be in the near-by town where I was stopping.

The curious aftermath of this experience was that

several of the Santo Domingos who participated in the decision against me came secretly to pose for me, each insisting that I never tell any other Santo Domingo that he had posed for his picture.

After leaving there I went on to Santa Fe, New Mexico, to the Indian School. There the Santo Domingo Indian girls, very fine subjects, posed for me.

The dances of the Pueblo Indians' ceremonies are of great significance to them, and they object to having strangers witness them. For example, I arrived at the pueblo of Jemez while the Indians were holding one of their important ceremonial dances in an open court. They immediately escorted me into a small dark room and insisted that I stay there until the dance was over.

Shortly before, just as the ceremonial dance was beginning, the United States mail stagecoach had arrived at the village. The Indians held up the coach, delaying it for four hours so that the driver could not see the dance while he was driving through the village. This act almost provoked war between the United States government and the Jemez pueblo. When the postmaster complained about the holding up of the mail, the Indians were warned that it must not happen again. They solved the problem by ingeniously rigging up a huge sheet between two poles. When during the next dance the mail coach arrived, two Indians walked alongside the stagecoach, carrying the sheet between the driver and the dancers, so that he could not see what was going on.

So far as I know there was only one white man permitted to witness a Jemez Indian ceremony. He had been made a medicine man for a most unusual reason. The Indians were digging an irrigation ditch when they encountered a boulder so large they could not remove it. This white man happened along about that time and obligingly blew the rock out of the way with dynamite. The white man's dynamite impressed them as being very potent medicine indeed, and they accepted him as one of their own people.

To me the most interesting of all the Pueblo Indians were the Hopis. They were known as the "peaceful people," and it was their proud boast that they had never waged an offensive war against their neighbors. Originally the Hopis were called "the Moqui Tribe." However, Moqui means "death" in their language, and the tribe changed its name to "Hopi" which means "life."

The Hopis still live in their compact villages built on three mesas or tablelands in eastern Arizona and western New Mexico, just as they did when the Spaniards first discovered them in 1540. At that time the gold hungry conquistadores thought they had found in the Hopi villages the fabulously rich seven cities of Cibola. Finding no gold among the Hopis, they returned to Mexico leaving these industrious natives to their quaint ways.

On the easternmost, or first mesa are the villages of Hano, Sichomovi, and Walapi. The people of the first mesa are the pottery makers. On the second mesa are the Mishnonghovi, Shipaulovi, and Shum-opavi. On the westernmost, or third mesa are the villages of Orabi, Hotemvilla, and Bacabi. Forty miles farther west is the village of Moenkopi which is the farming center for Oraibi. On the second and third mesas live the basket makers and rug weavers of Hopiland.

All of the Hopis except the residents of Hano, speak one language. Tradition has it that the people of Hano are Tewas. Originally they lived farther to the south in New Mexico, and were famed as war-riors. A century ago when the Hopis were being continuously robbed by the marauding Navajos and Apaches, the Tewas were invited to come there and live among them to act as guards against invasion. Since that time the Hopis have lived in peace. Being skillful pottery makers, the Tewas brought their art with them and are still the leaders in this craft.

I lived among the Hopis for many months. Never have I known a more charming, hospitable, and peace-loving people.

Several years prior to my arrival, the government, in the interest of good health, offered to build the stone walls of some new homes if the Hopis would agree to move down from the mesas to the lowlands. The Great White Father even agreed to put on tin roofs, to build floors and doors and windows in the new pueblos, and to furnish them with beds, stoves, chairs, and tables. Many of the Indians accepted this offer of furnished homes, and a number of them were built at Polacca, Arizona. But few of the Hopis

Store, barn, sheep corral, and residence of J. L. Hubbells, Ganado, Arizona, 1912.

Si-we-ka, Pueblo, 1898.

lived in the new houses. Instead they rented them to tourists and lived on the proceeds. I rented one of these houses for five dollars a month, and converted it into a comfortable studio. The house was just as the government had built it, except that the springs to the beds were gone. When I complained about this, the Hopi owner naively explained that he needed the bed springs to dry peaches in the sun.

Hopi life is typical of the best Pueblo traditions. Since I spent more time among the Hopis than among the other Pueblo tribes, I will try to give a word picture of it in detail, but living conditions in the other Pueblo villages are almost identical.

Life is hard, wrested from the barren soils of the southwestern deserts. It is a strange enigma indeed that the greatest advance towards civilization made by any primitive American people was achieved by the Pueblos. And of all the Pueblo peoples, the Hopis were the most advanced and prosperous.

As the result of repeated droughts, the Hopis had learned, like the ancient Egyptians, to store their grain against the dry years. They had no buffalo herds, fish-bearing streams, nor food-yielding wilderness in which to forage. Theirs was a harsh, unfriendly land which produced only when the weather conditions were exceptionally good. Usually the Hopis stored enough grain to last at least two years, in case of emergency.

Their lands for growing crops had been handed down from generation to generation for hundreds of years. Their farms were the joint property of the people of the village. Each village had its own farm lands, some of them quite distant. I was told that the men who farmed the lands belonging to the village of Moenkopi sometimes ran forty miles to their work in the morning, worked all day in the burning sun, then ran forty miles back home at night. This gives but an idea of the difficulties under which this amazing people carried on their agriculture.

Their principal crop was corn. Because of the frequent sandstorms, Hopis had to be very careful about the planting of their corn. First they would dig a hole in the sand, place a few grains in the hole, then build a fortification of dirt around the hill on the side from which the prevailing winds blew. This protected the young shoots from the sandstorms and by the time the corn grew above the fortification sandstorm time had passed.

That did not end the Hopi's worries over his cornfield. Crows and ground rats and other wild life hovered about waiting for a chance to eat the corn stalks. At the edge of each field a hut was built and there a Hopi stayed all day long watching for invaders. If bird or beast entered his field or that of his neighbors he stood sentinel to drive them away.

Corn was raised in three colors: red, yellow, and blue. They also grew many squashes and melons, and raised the finest peaches I ever ate. It was a custom among these people to allot each peach tree to a girl whose duty it was to care for the tree from childhood on as long as she lived.

Each Hopi village had its flock of turkeys. Curiously these were not raised for food, but for their feathers which were highly prized in ceremonial rites. Just before the big dances these turkeys presented an odd appearance strutting around with their tail feathers plucked. Many Hopi villages had their flocks of eagles which were captured young and raised in cages. They, too, were prized for their feathers.

In many ways the Hopi villages, like those of the other Pueblo Indians, were women's worlds. The weaker sex seemed to dominate the affairs of each pueblo. The women owned the property, including the pueblo itself. The family line was traced through the women. They had the final say so in most village affairs. Those who know the Pueblos say that it is the conservatism of the women of these tribes that is largely responsible for the lack of change in the four centuries that the Pueblos have been exposed to the white man's civilization.

The men were the farmers in each Hopi village. They were the warriors if the village was attacked. They conducted the ceremonial dances by which the Hopis propitiated their gods. The women, on the other hand, took charge of the food when it was produced, and stored it. They were the cooks, the pottery and basket makers, and the rug weavers. It always seemed to me that in spite of the fact that they were the bosses of the pueblo, the Hopi women took on much more of the work than did the men.

The most important job was that of grinding the corn into fine meal. This was done by pulverizing the

grain between two stones. It was a tedious operation
and it required a long time to get a little meal. The
little Hopi girls were started at this job as soon as
they were old enough to hold a grinding stone in their
hands. When they were grinding corn they would
sing, and all had sweet voices.

As soon as they were in their teens they learned to
make a bread called "pike." Many times I have
watched them at this fascinating operation. Their
stove consisted of a flat stone two feet long and one
foot wide. It was propped up at each corner with
smaller stones. Underneath it a fire was built. The
corn meal was mixed with water and lye, to make a
batter. When the stone was heated just right they
spread this batter over it with their hands. It cooked
very quickly and when it was done it was removed
from the hot stone in sheets as thin as paper. It
ranged in color from bluish black to pink.

I found pike very nourishing and healthful. When
rolled up it was most convenient to dunk into coffee
or soup. I became very fond of it until I saw the dogs
lying on the warm stones.

When I first arrived at Polacca I enjoyed the corn
bread made by the natives. But I enjoyed it, too, only
until I saw them make it. A group of Hopi women
would gather around a large bowl. They filled their
mouths with corn meal and began to chew. When the
meal was thoroughly mixed with saliva each woman
would deposit her contribution in the bowl. When a
sufficient amount had been accumulated it was put
in the oven to bake.

It is a well-known fact that saliva mixed with corn meal sweetens it in a chemical change. Many primitive people have used this method. I must admit that the Hopi corn bread was tasty, but after witnessing its preparation, I could no longer stomach it.

The Hopis were among the finest cooks I found in my years among the Indians. I never ate better corn, soup, or meats than those which they prepared. They were particularly skillful at cooking mutton.

While I was staying with the Indians, the government issued cattle to the various Indian tribes on the reservations. It was the custom to deliver them on the hoof. The Indians would shoot the steers, and as soon as an animal fell, men, women, and children rushed in to butcher it. This was a bloody sight. First the Indians would cut out the liver, dip it in the gall bladder, and eat it raw. In no time at all their hands and faces and clothes were covered with blood.

The Hopis had an ingenious way of catching small fowl known as winter birds. They tied several loops of horsehair to a stick about a yard long and placed it where the birds congregated on the snow. The birds invariably managed to get their feet tangled in the loops of horsehair and then the Hopi boys caught them. Pulling the quill from one of the tail feathers, the Hopi would pierce the snow bird's gizzard, killing it instantly. These little birds were roasted over hot coals, stringing about a dozen on a stick, then they were laid away for future consumption.

The climate was hot in the summer, and quite cold

in winter in most of the Hopi villages. But as a rule, the little Hopi children went around as naked in the winter as they did in the summer. I spent December, January, February, and March at Polacca, and saw children up to six years of age naked, playing in the snow. When they got cold they ran into the house.

As a consequence of the cold, the Hopi Indians could keep cooked food for a long time; likewise the melons, which they kept from one season to another. They had a trick for opening watermelons with their thumbs. They would make a nick at each end and then drop the melon to the ground from a height of about two feet. Invariably it would split lengthwise, exactly in the center. If a visitor were present when the melon was cracked, the Hopi would hand him one half and eat the other half himself. An accepted Hopi custom was to use the fingers to scoop out the center. Then rolled-up pike was used to sop up the juice.

The Hopi Indian women had likewise elected themselves to be beasts of burden. One of their principal jobs was carrying water to their homes on the mesa. At Polacca the pueblo is seven hundred feet above the surrounding territory. All the water they had was carried up the trail by the women in big earthen jars on their backs. Many times I have seen little Laguna girls playing games on their way back from the water hole, meanwhile carrying earthen jars on their heads without losing a drop of water.

The Hopis told me that they had known the art of weaving rugs, belts, and material for their clothes since ancient times. They told me that a dress

woven by a Hopi woman would last for a lifetime
with all kinds of wear. Among some of the Pueblo
tribes the men had taken up rug weaving and had
become very skillful at it.

From the Tewas the Hopis had learned the art of
making pottery that was artistic and decorative as
well as useful. The finest pottery of all, I believe, was
made by a Tewa woman named Nam-pay-a. The
Tewas had long since learned to develop colors for
their pottery by pulverizing different colored stones.
Green they obtained by allowing water to stand in
tin vessels until verdegris formed, and yellow from
boiling the yellow desert flowers.

In pottery making as well as in basketry each tribe
had its characteristic designs which were continuously repeated. One tribe, for example, made a jet
black pottery with a beautiful gloss. For a long time
it was a mystery how they obtained this beautiful
finish. One day I had the opportunity of seeing them
do it. They burned damp straw which gave off clouds
of black smoke. By glazing the pottery in this slow
heat they gave it the beautiful ebony finish so highly
prized in this ware.

The Zunis were the most skillful of the Pueblos in
making jewelry. They made unusually beautiful
shell beads by breaking sea shells into small pieces
about the size of a dime. They punched holes in these
pieces and strung them on wires. After this they
would roll the shells on a stone with their hands until
each bead was round and smooth. Then they strung

the shell beads with others made from turquoise and whole shells.

The Zunis also made elaborately designed blankets which they wore in their numerous ceremonies. If any dancer should happen to stumble or fall during the ceremony, the blanket was never used again and would be sold for a low price.

In their spare time the Hopis often busied themselves carving small images of wood which they called "katcins," or gods. These were originally made for the Hopi children, but when the Hopis discovered that they could be sold to tourists, a thriving industry in wood carving was developed.

I found the Hopis as well as the other Pueblos very fond of music. Many of them, especially the girls, had wonderful singing voices.

The Hopis seemed particularly fond of their children. One time I was standing in a trading post when a Hopi father and his little girl came into the store. The little girl took a fancy to a toy in the shop. The Hopi father lacked the money to buy the toy. Rather than have the youngster disappointed, he took off his moccasins, left them with the storekeeper as security, and went away barefooted, his little girl happily clutching the toy.

As soon as the Hopi girls' hair became long enough, it was done up on each side of her head in a flat knot representing a squash blossom. This was a difficult thing to do, and once done the hair was kept that way for a long time. However, as soon as the girl married, the squash blossoms were supposed to fade, and then the hair was taken down and made into two long braids which hung down in front of her shoulders. These were the only two styles of head dress used among the Hopi women. The men usually wore their hair cropped just above their shoulders with a band around their foreheads.

The Hopis never punished their children, yet they seemed to extract the greatest obedience from them by kindness alone. The discipline of the youngsters was amazing. I painted pictures of several of these little Hopi children and they sat as patiently as did the older people.

One day Quen-Chow-a, a Hopi girl eighteen years old, was sitting for me. She sat still so long that the strain became too great and before I realized that she was uncomfortable she had fainted away. I was wondering how I could revive her when her mother who happened to be with her that day rushed outside, and returned with a handful of sand which she rubbed over her daughter's stomach. This was a new treatment to me, but apparently it was very effective because the girl recovered consciousness immediately.

During this period I decided that the little North American Indian was perhaps the happiest child in the world. For some deep reason known only to the simple, primitive heart, the Indian father and mother trained their children in psychological principles which only recently the white man has discovered.

Modern psychologists say, "Be slow and gentle with children; suddenness, either mental or physical, will confuse them. Let their life fall into a routine. Let them feel they are part of the family. Let them develop as individuals, and do not repress, but guide their natural interests." This was the policy of the Indians as I observed them.

Nowhere were children more charmingly treated than among the Pueblo Indians, for example. It was rare to hear a Pueblo child cry or to hear him quarrel with his playmates. I think I never saw a Pueblo Indian strike or punish a child. And the little people were polite, gentle, and happy.

How did the Indian parents accomplish this miracle? First by affection. Then, both men and women, young and old, always had time for the youngsters. The interests of the children were woven smoothly into the routine of the home. If the mother was making pottery, she gave the little child a piece of clay to work with. Then she never said, "No, no, you're doing it wrong. Make your pot this way." She simply let the child learn by trial and error and by watching her skillful hands.

When the pots were ready to be fired, a whole host of children showed up with ears of blue corn. The firing was done out-of-doors, without a kiln, by means of a sort of bonfire. After the blaze died down, the mother always had time to shell the blue corn and rake some of the embers into the sand, so that the children could drop the kernels among the hot coals and pop them.

Little girls were encouraged to balance on their heads little pots which were cracked or had turned out badly in the fire. If they broke the pots, nothing was said. Soon they would bring up water from the river or the pump, though among the Hopi Indians the older women did most of the water carrying.

They were very saving with water. For instance, I have seen a mother bathe her baby with water in her mouth, letting the water drop on the infant's body.

Every Pueblo child could dance almost as soon as he could walk. At sundown it was common to see a Pueblo father, after a long day's work in the fields, pick up a tiny thing perhaps only three months old, and hold the baby carefully against his breast while he chanted a weird Indian song and went through the steps of a dance. Indian rhythms were thus literally danced into the babies.

When the Pueblo Indians put on a dance, the tiny tots followed along after their elders, dressed in ceremonial clothes just like the grown-ups. They brought up the rear of a long line of dancers, patting out the rhythm with tiny feet in buckskin shoes. Seldom did they err in the tempo, though the detail of the step might be a little vague. But again, no one corrected them or criticized them. It was assumed that they had their part in the tribal ceremony, and that they were doing well. They learned in their own way.

The life of the entire pueblo was slow and gentle and quiet. The bright sun rose, work in the fields and in the house went on. There was clay to play with. There were playmates and dogs and cats. And one day was much like another. Adults spoke to each other quietly, courteously. An Indian's voice is seldom raised; seldom is he inconsiderate in his speech. These habits are quickly picked up by children.

There was always a grandfather or aunt or big sister ready to cradle the sleepy child; always an old man singing an ancient song or telling an ancient tale out in the plaza, in the shade of the house. Sleepy babies swung happily in cradle swings suspended from the roof beams. They were securely tied in, and one good push kept them swinging for many minutes.

It seemed to me no wonder that Indian children were both happy and good.

But the Hopi youngsters, like their parents, were not above playing tricks, even on the "Witch Man."

One day I was preparing to eat an apple when a Hopi boy reached up to me and said, "Oh, you handsome man. Give me that apple."

At Polacca the Indian agent, Major Williams, always brought a pail of candy for the children when he visited the pueblo. He was very fond of Hopi youngsters and they of him. However, that did not keep them from playing jokes on him.

One day in mid-winter half a dozen little Hopi girls came into my studio while Major Williams was there. They were all barefooted.

"What!" exclaimed the Major. "You are walking barefooted in the snow?"

The girls did not explain to him that they had purposely removed their shoes before entering the studio. A short time after the Major left, a shipment of shoes arrived, a pair for every child in the pueblo.

One day a little Hopi boy came to me and said that his teacher had told him to learn a piece to recite in school. He wanted me to teach him something. I scratched my head and could think of nothing but "Peter, Peter, Pumpkin Eater," so I told him that. He learned the piece all right, but he could not pronounce the words very well. As he spoke it, it sounded like "Pater, Pater, Punkin Ater." The next day I received word from his teacher that if I couldn't do better than that I had better stick to my art.

While I learned a few words of the Hopi language, they were largely terms dealing with food, and those needed, to tell my subjects when to rest. There were times when I wished that I knew the language well. One of these times was while I was at Polacca. A little Indian girl came to me one day and asked me to accompany her. She led me to a big rock and we sat down. She seemed to be in great trouble and wanted me to help her. She talked to me earnestly for more than an hour. I could not understand a word she was saying but I listened intently. Every so often she would be so overcome that she would cry. All I could say was "How-o," meaning "Is that so?" She would answer most piteously "Oh-ee," which means, "Yes, that is so." I have often wondered what it was all about and why she would unburden her heart to a white man.

I once took two Hopi boys on a trip from Polacca to Holbrook, Arizona, via Keam Canyon, about 125 miles. I had a buckboard and a team of horses. We camped out in the open and it was a revelation to me to find out what excellent cooks these two youngsters were and how easily they could fix up a comfortable camp out on the desert.

One day we came to a ravine which it seemed impossible to cross. It looked as though our journey were over. The Hopis got out and cut all the underbrush they could find. They partly filled in the ravine, then unhitched the horses and let the wagon down by hand. They coaxed the horses down into the ravine, rehitched them, and then with much shouting and pushing managed to get the rig up the other bank.

In Holbrook one of the horses, never having seen a train before, broke loose and ran away. One of the Hopi boys set out to trail him and in a short time he brought the horse back.

We had run out of meat on the trip and were obliged to get along without enough food for the last day. At Holbrook I took the boys into a Chinese restaurant for breakfast. The price of the breakfast was fifty cents. The Hopis wanted to know if that meant they could eat all they wanted. The Chinaman, who was both cook and waiter, told them they could. They were still eating when I left them to go down the street to tend to some business. On my way back to the restaurant I met a man who wanted to know if the Indian boys in the Chinese restaurant were my charges. I told him they were.

"You better hurry up," he said. "They are eating the Chink out of house and home."

They were still eating when I entered. The Chinaman was laughing.

"Little Indian boys velly big appetite," he said, passing them another stack of hot cakes.

These Hopi boys had never seen a locomotive close up. When they finally finished eating, I took them over to look at a new one the Santa Fe had just received. The engineer took a liking to the little Indians and took them all over the locomotive, explaining carefully how it worked. The boys were delighted, but what intrigued them most was when they put their eyes down on the rails and squinted up the line. They were trying to figure out why the rails met in the distance instead of running parallel.

The Hopis invariably showed a childlike interest in all my personal belongings and affairs. I subscribed for a Chicago paper while I was living in Polacca. The political cartoons particularly intrigued them. I remember one cartoon which showed a woman on horseback pursued by a bunch of cowboys on horseback, all armed to the teeth with daggers and pistols. The Hopis assumed that this was a picture of a real occurrence and wanted to know what manner of men were these that they would chase a woman that way. For the sake of the white man's reputation I was obliged to give them an elaborate explanation of the picture, but even then they could not understand why a band of armed men would want to chase a helpless woman.

Another cartoon showed a rooster dressed up in coat, pants, and hat, smoking a pipe and carrying a cane under his wing. This picture puzzled them beyond words. They talked about it so much and so many of them came to see the picture of "the rooster that smoked," that I finally gave them the paper to get rid of them.

I soon learned in working among the Indians never to leave my portraits uncovered during my absence. The Indians were unable to distinguish pictures of birds and elk's teeth from the real article, and frequently they would attempt to pick them off the canvas, sometimes ruining my work. Somehow they couldn't realize that paintings were paintings.

When I was at Polacca, I painted two pictures of the Snake Dance. Always when the dance is in progress some old Hopi sprinkles sacred meal on all the dancers. The last picture I had painted of the Snake Dance was on my easel, not quite dry. I noticed a Hopi woman looking at the painting up close. Just in time I caught her as she was about ready to sprinkle real meal over the wet paint. Of course she had no intention of ruining the picture, but merely wished to give it luck.

One day I was painting the belle of the Hopi village, a young woman recently married, while her husband sat on the bed in back of me. She could speak English, but he could not, so I payed very little attention to him. When I looked around, I discovered him squeezing paint out of the tubes in papers to take home. He had paint all over his hands, and I resolved to give him a good scare. I hurriedly told his wife to tell him to wash his hands immediately, because the paint was deadly poison and would kill him. We rushed around with water and soap and had him scrubbing his hands furiously. Meantime I pretended a great anxiety. Finally the paints were removed and I expressed great relief. Evidently this Indian told the others of the tribe, because after that I had no more trouble of that kind.

One day I was painting a portrait of Sah-ah-lok-o, an old Hopi woman. While she was posing, an old friend of hers came in. The day was hot and he began shedding his clothes piece by piece until he stood in nothing but a breech cloth. She seemed not in the least way embarrassed by his disrobing. The day being so warm, I wished that the artist "Many-Brushes" could do the same, but I was no Indian.

In every Pueblo village I found one or more churches. Some of them were old churches built a century or more ago by the early Catholic missionaries. Some were newer churches built by the Protestants. Indians had adopted some of the missionaries' teachings, but they clung to their own ideas of how the world was made and of the hereafter.

The Zunis had a legend about Thunder Mountain which was similar to that of Noah in the Bible. They believed that when the flood came, inundating all the country, their tribe built a refuge on the top of this mountain where they remained a long time. To prove this they pointed to the remains of a village still to be seen near the mountain top.

One zealous missionary among the Zunis told them the Bible story of the creation. He told them that God made man from adobe and that by taking a rib from Adam's side He made woman. At this point the Zunis refused to listen any longer.

"What kind of man could He make from adobe and what kind of woman from a rib and how could she bear children?" they asked.

The missionary was never able to answer this satisfactorily to them and that ended his efforts to preach to them.

At Acoma, New Mexico, where I went one day by team, about twenty-five miles from Laguna, New Mexico, I saw a fine old church, and as it was near Christmas time, the Indians were decorating the church for Christmas festivities. I went into the church, and saw twelve large oil paintings as large as doors. Eleven of them had been ruined by dew damp, but one of the paintings was in good condition. It was a fine picture of a saint holding the infant Christ in his hand, and had been painted by Moro, a great Spanish artist. The next day I spoke to Mr. Marmon, who lived at Laguna, about the painting. He told me the Laguna Indians had taken the painting away from the Acomas, but that later on the Acoma Indians had succeeded in getting the picture back. I wrote to the Smithsonian Institute in Washington about the painting, and they replied that they knew all about it, and would give forty thousand dollars for it.

When the Smithsonian wrote me about the painting, they said they wished that Catlin (a well known artist who painted Indians long before I was born) had painted more portraits of Indians like I was painting. Catlin devoted more of his time to painting the different dances the Indians gave then. Some of the dances he painted have been stopped by the government because of their cruelty. These paintings are now priceless. When I was at the Sac and Fox Agency, Chief Keokuk posed for a portrait for me. He had on the wall in his comfortable home, a print taken from a picture that Catlin had painted of his father dressed in the Sac and Fox Indian costume. Keokuk, Iowa, was named after Keokuk's father.

A little later I went to Acometa, New Mexico, where there was a young Acoma Indian who was well educated and could speak good English. I told him to try to use his influence to get the painting; that the forty thousand dollars could be divided among the Acoma Indians. He asked me to give him the address of a store where he could purchase some books on American history.

In due time I arrived at St. Michaels, Arizona, where the Franciscan monks lived. They could not have been nicer to me than they were; in fact, they were the same to all who came there. They had a school for Navajo Indians. No missionaries were doing better work for the Indians than they were. They had a large farm where they raised all they ate, had pigs, chickens, cattle, and other stock. I spoke to the Fathers about the painting in the church at Acoma. They told me the painting belonged to the

Catholic Church. Later on I was told the painting met the same fate as the other eleven pictures.

Frequently the good people at the Sunday school back home packed up batches of clothing and other articles which were sent out to the missionaries for distribution among the Indians. Often the natives were at a loss to know how to use some of these contributions. While I was at Polacca, a large shipment of warm clothing and toys was distributed. Among the goods were a dozen flannel night gowns, a tall plugged hat, and a swallow-tailed coat with a vest. On the following Sunday morning several of the squaws wore flannel nightgowns to church. A chief named Ho-mo-vi fell heir to the plug hat and the swallow-tailed coat with the vest. Lacking trousers to go with them, he painted his bare legs yellow, donned the rest of the outfit, and after church came to my studio where he earnestly besought me to paint his portrait.

All of the Pueblos are stocky people of short stature, but of great physical strength. The men are known for their prowess as runners. The Hopi men often ran from twenty to forty miles to work and back again in the evening.

While I was among the Zunis I saw a unique barefooted race over a twenty-five-mile course. Much money was bet on this race. Each runner carried two sticks painted different colors. As he ran, the runner picked up the sticks with his toes and threw them in front of him with his feet. Even if the stick fell in the midst of a cactus plant, the runner was obliged to pick it out with his toes. The Hopi had a similar race using stones instead of sticks.

The agent at the Zuni pueblo told me that the Indian who carried the mail from the agency to the railroad, a distance of thirty-five miles, made the round trip on foot in twelve hours.

One day I noticed in the home of a Zuni a gold-headed cane bearing the inscription "A. Lincoln." It excited my curiosity and I made inquiries. The Indians told me that many years ago a group of their forefathers journeyed to the center of the white man's land to visit the Great White Father. They had been entertained at the Big White House and Lincoln had given each of them a gold-headed cane to take home. The canes had been handed down from father to son for generations and were held in great veneration by all Pueblos.

Once, while a delegation of Zunis was in Washington, the Barnum circus came to town. P. T. Barnum invited the Indians to see the spectacle from a special box, and asked if he might sit among them to observe their comments. They watched every detail and conversed in their own tongue. Finally Barnum asked the interpreter what they were saying. Their talk was entirely of the trapeze performers who were hurtling through the air. The Zunis were fearful lest they should fall and get hurt.

After the show, the great showman gave the Zunis a fine dinner and offered to let them take home anything they had seen at the circus—an elephant, a cage of lions, a steam caliope, or anything they

wanted. The Zunis held a council. What they wanted
most, they said, was a set of the circus billboard
posters, so that they could show their tribe what they
had seen.

The Hopis would never believe me when I told
them what a lot of white people there were in the
world. While I was among them, a delegation of
Hopis went to Washington. They decided to count
white men and see whether or not I was lying. The
Santa Fe gave them a private car, in which the
Hopis stationed a man at each window to count white
people. From Holbrook to Albuquerque, they had no
trouble, but by the time they reached Kansas City the
white people were so thick they decided to count
houses. They counted houses all the way to Chicago,
and then began counting towns. That kept them busy
until they reached Washington, where they held a
powwow and decided that Many-Brushes had not
lied to them, after all.

The greatest surprise I had among the Pueblos
came one day when I was sitting in my studio at
Polacca writing letters. A white man entered and I
greeted him asking him where he came from. He
looked at me questioningly.

"Right here," he said. "I am a Hopi Indian."

I studied him more closely. His skin complexion
was lighter than my own. His hair was yellow and
his eyes were pink. He was a Hopi albino.

Later on I became well acquainted with him and
found him well educated, able to speak both English
and Hopi. His wife was a Hopi girl and their chil-

dren were as dark as those of any other native. After
that I was always on the lookout for another albino,
but among the 128 Indian tribes I visited, I never
found another "white Indian."

DANCING FOR THE GODS

All Indian tribes love ceremony involving religious dances, but none more than the Pueblos, who evolve a rite for every occasion of life. The Hopi people, in particular, were devoted to their ceremonies, the most famous of which was the Snake Dance.

Although most of the dances of the Pueblo Indians were forbidden to white men's eyes, I was permitted to witness many of those of the Hopis, as I had been accepted as one of them. The Hopi dances were the most elaborate of the rites practiced by the Pueblos. Features of the Hopi dances were practiced by the other Indians of the Southwest—even relics of the Snake Dance.

To appreciate these dances, you must regard them not as spectacles of entertainment, but in all seriousness. In a sense the Hopis were nature worshippers. Their dances dramatized their earnest supplications to their gods. They were dances of thanks, and dances pleading for rain, which in the Southwestern desert was life itself.

Adobe Building, near the Pima Reservation at Sacaton, Arizona, 1942.

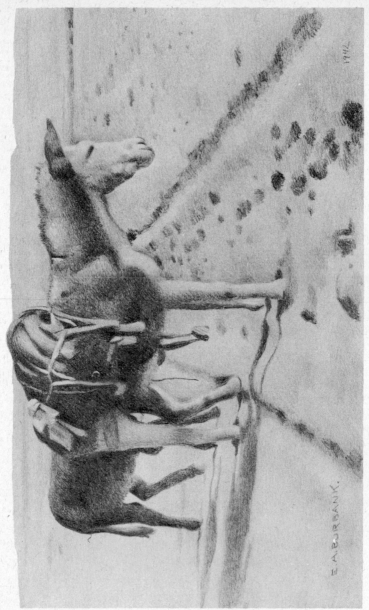

Burros, 1942.

Desert Mailbox.

An Indian Stufa, or Meeting Place, Isleta, New Mexico.

He-patina, Shrine of the Zunis. The Zunis believed this place to be the center of the earth, which in their view was flat.

Ho-mo-vi.

Wick-ah-te-wah, Hopi Indian in Snake Dance Costume, 1898.

Sah-ah-lock-o, Hopi Woman in Ceremonial Robes.

Wickey, Moqui, 1898.

Shu-pe-la, Moqui, 1898.

Kopeley, Moqui, 1898.

Ton-had-dle, 1898.

I was eager to paint the Pueblo Indians in as many elaborate ceremonial costumes as possible. I had no success among the Zunis, the Santo Domingos, and the other tribes who held their dances in great secrecy. Good luck awaited me when I arrived among the Hopis.

It was fortunate that the head of the Snake Clan among the Hopis at the time of my arrival was Kopeley, one of the most remarkable Indians I ever met. Kopeley was about twenty-five years old, a man of vigorous character and attractive personality. He was kindly disposed toward the white men and had won their respect by his industry and ability. Although he was conservative in character, he was open-minded toward innovations, welcoming every opportunity to improve the lot of his people.

So when I proposed to Kopeley that he let me paint him in the complete ceremonial costume of the Hopi Snake Dance, he agreed, after due deliberation. As he posed for his portrait, he was one of the most impressive figures that it has been my lot to encounter.

Kopeley wore on his head a bunch of eagle feathers stained red with sesquioxide of iron, the prescribed pigment of a warrior. To these feathers were attached those of a bluebird. The latter were symbolical of certain mystic adventures in the underworld from which the Snake Clan is supposed to have sprung.

The Snake chief's face was blackened. His cheeks were painted with iron. His chin was smeared with resin to represent a rain cloud. His kilt and buckskin thongs were stained red. Red was also the color used by the Snake priests to decorate their bodies.

He wore a necklace of badger claws to which were attached marine shells. The bandolier that hung over his right shoulder was decorated with stone arrow points and small seashells. To it were attached small pellets of clay which had been dipped in a medicine used by the Hopis to protect themselves from the bites of rattlesnakes.

In his right hand Kopeley carried a snake whip consisting of a wooden handle to which were bound turkey feathers. In the Snake Dance he used this whip to wave before the eyes of the reptiles. It confused them and caused them to uncoil when they had assumed a position for striking.

All of the objects worn by Kopeley in his Snake Dance costume had a special significance. They were not mere decorations, but were there for a purpose which only the Snake priests could appreciate.

Kopeley had inherited his position as chief from his uncle a few years before. He was the son of the oldest woman in the Snake Clan at Walpi. He was married and had one daughter.

The young chief took his responsibilities with great earnestness. When he learned that the Zunis were in the midst of an epidemic of smallpox, he considered it his duty to visit them and offer such help as he could. He did this over the protests of his friends. As was to be expected, Kopeley himself contracted smallpox and died soon after his return to Polacco.

Several other Hopis who had handled Kopeley's

effects contracted the disease, and the government finally was obliged to send soldiers to destroy everything that was left of his possessions to check the epidemic.

Kopeley's untimely death deprived the Hopis of a remarkable leader who, had he lived the normal span of life, might have become one of the greatest Indian chiefs of American history.

After Kopeley's death, his brother Harry took his place as the head chief of the Snake Clan. His mother, Sah-o-lok-o, continued to make the remarkable medicine which the Snake dancers drank after the ceremony to counteract the effect of being bitten by the snakes. The formula of the medicine was a secret which the government tried in vain for many years to secure.

Sah-o-lok-o was a remarkable woman and I felt privileged to paint her portrait. She had an unusually fine mentality and like her son was open-minded to new ideas. She was known as Woman-Chief of the Basket Dance.

While I was at Polacca, Sah-o-lok-o became converted in the Baptist Church. After that she refused to make medicine for the Snake dancers any more. This caused much disagreement between her and her husband, a fine old man named Shu-pe-la who belonged to the Snake Clan. It brought her into disfavor with her son Harry who had become chief of the clan after the death of his brother. But the old squaw took her conversion to Christianity seriously and refused to make medicine for the Snake Dance.

Shu-pe-la was the head of the Indian order corresponding in a way to the Masons. It was an order of great honor and influence among the Hopis. Once I was privileged to witness one of their important ceremonies.

The ritual was put on at the request of the Smithsonian Institute who had sent Doctor Fewkes to make a record of it. We descended a ladder into the kiva—a cave about twenty-five feet below the surface of the earth. Before we entered, Shu-pe-la, who stood at the head of the ladder, pledged each of us not to reveal what occurred during the ceremony, which lasted all night long.

The Kiva was beautifully decorated for the occasion. They had an altar at one end suggesting that of a Catholic Church.

One of the performers was dressed to represent an eagle. On his face he wore an eagle-like mask. On his feet were moccasins having eagle claws. His arms represented the wings of an eagle. The costumes and the lighting produced a most startling effect, one that will remain in my memory to the end of my life.

Witnessing this ceremony was almost my undoing among the Hopis. On the following day several members of the order were watching me work in my studio when I guilelessly asked one of them who it was that wore the eagle costume on the night before. I wanted to ask him to pose for me.

As soon as the question was out of my mouth, a Tewa, who was in the group, rose and hurriedly left the studio. The other Indians broke into an uproar.

Among their outcries I distinguished one word, "Kahl-lone-lo-my." I knew that meant "not good."

When the uproar subsided, one of the Hopis informed me I had divulged a secret of their order and that I would shortly swell up and burst.

Next morning about five o'clock I heard a commotion at my door. I was still intact, but on opening the door encountered Shu-pe-la, greatly excited. He stamped his foot and talked so loud and so fast I could not understand a word he said. I sent for his son Harry, who could speak English. Harry explained that his father was so upset because I had revealed one of the secrets of the order. Through Harry I explained that I had no thought nor intention of revealing secrets. I proposed that inasmuch as the Tewa was the only one in my studio who was not a member of the order, I would go to him and pledge him not to tell anyone what he had heard. This calmed the old man down and the next day I took the Tewa to Shu-pe-la, where the former promised never to mention the incident in my studio.

As time went on Shu-pe-la relented and became one of my very good friends, actually posing for me, and wearing the eagle costume about which I had inquired. Harry, his son, posed in the Snake Dance costume. Among the other picturesque Hopis whom I painted in their ceremonial costumes was O-bah, who was dressed to represent the rain god whom the Hopis called "Humis." I was also privileged to paint the Divine Mask, which the Hopis considered the strongest kind of medicine. They assured me the magic gourds alone were good for a shower of rain any time.

One day while I was painting Ho-mo-vi in the secret Snake Dance costume, Wickey, a big, six-foot Indian who was deaf, came into the studio and harangued Ho-mo-vi not to pose for me. He warned us that if I continued with the portrait we would both swell up and burst.

Wickey was an important man among the Hopis, being the head chief of the Antelope Clan. When he finally left the room, Ho-mo-vi asked me not to let him come in again. But the next day was so warm that we had to keep the door open. Ho-mo-vi saw Wickey coming and called out to me to close the door. Before I could put down my pallet and close the door, Wickey stuck his foot inside. He recited the same warning as on the previous days, only much louder this time. I shouted to him that I not only intended to paint Ho-mo-vi, but that I planned to paint him, Wickey, as well in his Antelope costume before I left. He stamped his foot and said, "Never."

To get Wickey's friendship I purchased a fine Navajo blanket for fifteen dollars and presented it to him. Wickey accepted the gift with some reluctance and I could see that a struggle was going on within him. But in a short time he came in to pose for me, wearing the costume of the Antelope Clan. Wickey's great ambition was to live to see a train of cars. Finally, he journeyed down to the railroad track ninety miles to Holbrook, and was walking along the track when a train overtook him and killed him. Because of his deafness, he did not hear it coming. So you might say that Wickey never did live to see a train.

The Snake Dance which has made the Hopi tribes famous the world over is presented on three different mesas. I have seen it on each of the three mesas. The only difference in the dance is that at Walpi the Hopis did not touch the snakes with their hands while they held them in their mouths. On the other mesas they did. The Snake Dance is an elaborate prayer for rain, which is as important as life itself to the Hopis. I once asked one of them what would happen if the dance failed to produce rain. He replied that it would mean that someone of them had not done his part correctly during the nine-day ceremony.

It is a strange but curious fact that shortly after the Snake Dance it invariably does rain throughout the Pueblo Indian country. So the Hopis have some reason for their faith in the efficacy of the Snake Dance.

They told me a legend which explained the origin of the dance.

One day long ago a small Hopi boy was watching the Colorado River when he asked his father where the water flowed.

"It flows a long ways until it runs into a deep hole," the father replied.

The boy asked his father to build him a boat and give him provisions so that he might follow the river into the deep hole. This the father did and the boy started on his journey.

After a long trip he landed in a great cave where an old woman came to him. She told the boy that she would turn herself into a spider, light on his ear, and tell him where to go.

The Spider Woman guided the boy through many dark caves until they came to one lined with snake-skins. In it the cave men were dancing the Snake Dance.

"Watch them closely," the Spider Woman told the boy. "Then return to your people and show them how to perform a dance."

She told him to return to his people and hold the dance once every two years. He was to dig a hole, cover it with a board, and as the dance continued, each dancer should stamp on the board with his feet so that those in the underworld would know that the dance was being performed.

For generations these instructions have been carried out by the Hopis to the last detail and to this day the dancers continue to stamp on the board as they perform their strange ceremony for rain.

Another legend of the Hopis states that the children of the marriage of the Snake hero and the Snake maid in ancient times were transformed into snakes. The snakes were regarded by the Hopis as earthly brothers. They were thought to be all-powerful in asking the water gods to bring rain.

The ceremony is said to represent an agreement between the Snake and the Antelope clans to hold a joint celebration of their respective rites which conflicted when the clans originally came together. As the prayers are dramatized, certain roles are assigned to Snakes, certain to the Antelopes.

The dance occurs once in two years about the twentieth of August. More than one hundred live snakes are used in the rites. Contrary to popular belief, no efforts are made to render the reptiles innocuous either by extraction of their fangs, or by the use of drugs.

Six days before the ceremony begins, the men in the Snake Clan go down to the plains and hunt snakes. I have gone with them and have seen them use their eagle feather wands to distract the snakes and keep them from coiling to spring. The snakes were put in bags and brought to the kiva where they were given a bath. Both bullsnakes and rattlesnakes are used without discrimination.

For nine days the priests of the Snake Clan never leave the kiva for any purpose. They eat and sleep with the snakes during that time. I was told that they place all the snakes on a table and as fast as the reptiles crawl off to the ground they are replaced on the table.

I do not know of any white man who ever witnessed what went on in the kiva. I was told that when the snakes were assembled the snake priests began to sing in a minor key. Their snake song charmed the reptiles as they raised their heads and listened to it. As the song became louder the snakes raised their heads higher, finally swaying with the music. As it became softer they relaxed again on the table. It was when the singing stopped that the snakes crawled off onto the floor.

When I was with the Ukiah Indians at Ukiah, California, I noticed a root hanging on the wall. Upon inquiring what it was for, I was told they chew the root and rub the saliva on their legs when they are gathering berries. It is offensive to rattlesnakes. I showed the root to Dr. Hudson in Ukiah, and he told me it was a fine stomach remedy every drugstore had.

I also showed the root to Harry Shupela, who was head chief of the Snake Dance at Walpi, Arizona. He told me the same root grew in their country; that they gathered it and boiled it and rubbed it on them during the nine-days' ceremony in the kiva. He said that no snake would bite them while they had it on, but that they did not use it in the Snake Dance ceremony.

At the end of the ninth day of ceremony in the kiva, the Antelope men came up the ladder. They were followed by members of the Snake Clan. Then began the only part of the ritual which the public has been privileged to see—the Snake Dance.

After all the dancers were assembled, the Snake men went to the bags where each reached in and pulled out a snake which he placed in his mouth. He began to dance, going around a big circle three times, each dancer stamping the board-covered hole as he passed it. If the snake dropped from his teeth, he picked it up and resumed his dance. If the snake coiled for striking, the gatherer touched it with his snake whip. During the dance, the Snake women continually sprinkled corn meal upon the dancers.

As each gatherer picked up a snake, it was handed to one of the Antelope men, usually about twenty in number, who gathered on each side of a tree transplanted in the court yard. One of the Snake men in the meantime drew a circle the size of a cartwheel upon the ground. Into this circle the Antelope men dumped all the snakes in a pile.

At a signal, the Snake men who had gathered around this circle seized several snakes apiece and ran in different directions from the mesa to the valley. There the snakes were given their freedom. They were to crawl off into the underworld to advise the rain gods that the Hopis needed moisture.

When the Snake men returned to the mesa they drank the snake medicine which caused them to vomit violently, and bathed in it. Although the formula was secret, I learned that one important ingredient is the juice of a small red bug.

The dancers were just as fearful of being bitten as any normal person would be, and all of them side-stepped a rattler if the reptile were coiled. Each dancer always carried a supply of medicine on hand to use at once in case he was bitten.

At one of the dances I noticed a boy ten years old who during the ceremony had been given a bull snake about six feet long. This snake had begun to coil around the youngster's neck like a scarf, and in the excitement no one noticed his predicament. I told one of the Snake men that the snake was strangling the lad. The Indian calmly uncoiled the reptile, gave it to the boy, and went on with his dance!

All of the members of the Snake Clan were sons of former Snake men, just as the offices in the Antelope Clan were handed down from father to son. Before they reached their teens the youngsters began to take part in the rites, preparing themselves for the day when they would become priests.

In the excitement of the occasion, it looked as though every dancer were following his own idea. But I learned later that each dancer had his special detail to perform in the ritual. The duty of Wick-ah-te-wah, for example, was to hold at the door of the kiva a bow to which a red fringe was attached, warning all outsiders not to enter. To Kah-kap-tee was assigned the task of collecting colored sand to make the Snake pictures of the prayer emblems. He painted his skin, curiously, with zigzag stripes representing lightning. I was told that before the dancers left the kiva on the ninth day, the snakes were allowed to crawl over Kah-kap-tee's sand pictures to destroy them. Thus they carried the message of the prayer to the underworld.

For many years the Hopis were very secretive about their Snake Dance, being fearful that the government agents would prohibit it. No pictures were made of the ceremony because the most important part of it was held just before dusk. At the conclusion of the dance thousands of visitors—not only white people, but Navajos, Apaches, and other Indians—were permitted to witness it. As the Snake men dashed off to deliver the reptiles to their homes, the Navajos invariably made a rush to gather up the sacred meal which the Hopi medicine women had distributed, believing that this meal would bring them good luck.

The Hopis had a ritual for every emergency. For the rare occasions when cloudbursts brought too much moisture and threatened to wash their crops away, they had a ceremony to retard the rains.

Once I witnessed this rite which they had not performed for more than forty years. The dancers dressed in odd-looking clothing and wore masks made from dried mud. The ceremony looked more like the play of children than anything else as the performers chased one another from roof to roof, jumping occasionally to the ground where they would roll in the mud until they were thoroughly coated with it.

The Hopis had another ceremony for the boys and girls who, upon reaching a certain age, had to be initiated into the tribe. When I had been living among them for some time I was invited to join in this ceremony.

There were about twenty boys and girls to be initiated. The rites were held in the kiva. As we entered, we passed two old men humming a tune. One of them, a very large Indian, was entirely nude. It was his duty to hold the child about to be initiated while the other Indian held a whip made of cactus, from which the thorns had been removed. Upon the floor of the kiva a cross had been painted. On top of this was a feather.

To another Indian was assigned the duty of summoning the children who stood at the top of the ladder with their mothers. The mother led her child forward and called out its name. The child came down the ladder and advanced to the cross, putting his or her foot on the feather, whereupon the man with the whip applied it until the blood ran.

After the first few applications of the whip some of the children were hard to catch. They darted about in the kiva and it was here that the nude Indian performed his role. His job was to catch them.

At the end of the ceremony the children were told that under no circumstances were they to tell what had happened, under the penalty of having their tongues cut out. Even I did not escape taste of the whip. I was required to bare my legs so that the Indian with the whip could give me several lashes, after which I, too, was warned not to make any pictures of this ceremony.

Before the dance part of the ceremony, an Indian made up in a hideous costume and known as Katcin-as, or the god of the Hopis, went from house to house begging food to be eaten by the several gods during the ceremony.

These gods were most outlandish figures. Some of them had on masks resembling crocodiles, with long teeth showing, and the jaws working up and down. Another I saw had a mask that looked like death, with great yellow eyes, long black hair, and whiskers. One carried a long butcher knife covered with blood, and a shepherd's crook to which was fastened several bones, and as he hit the ground with this crook it made a ghastly sound.

As these gods went from house to house, the leader rapped on the door and asked for food. The contribution was first handed by the Indians to a little child who was forced to give the food to these hideous visitors. The gods always wanted more food than the squaw cared to give. If she refused, they frequently became threatening, waving the bloody butcher knife.

Several times I watched this weird performance. Often I have seen the squaw place her hands over her child's eyes so that the youngster could not see the hideous god to whom it was giving food. Sometimes when this was not done, the child became so frightened it went into hysterics. The Hopis told their children that these were gods from another world.

In one of the Hopi ceremonies—the Butterfly Dance—the little children participated. They were dressed as symbols of corn, rainbows, rain clouds, and flowers. Little children just starting to school took parts quite complicated. Sometimes the youngsters were taken from school for three weeks before the dance to rehearse their parts.

On the morning of the dance the two tiniest girls and the two smallest boys who were able to do the dance began to dance just as the sun rose. After a half hour of dancing they went down to a kiva where they shed their costumes, which were then donned by

the next oldest quartet. Every half hour the costume
was changed, and the dance went on all day. By sun-
set the oldest unmarried boys and girls were still
dancing.

The Hopis had an unusual arrangement when a
boy and girl fell in love with each other. The boy
went to live with the girl's parents for several weeks,
during which time the elders decided if the two were
well suited to each other. If the decision were against
them, there was no wedding, but if the girl's parents
accepted him as a son-in-law an elaborate wedding
ceremony lasting several days followed. So, in spite
of their conservatism, the Hopis had trial marriages
years before the most advanced of our own people
hit upon the idea.

As was to be expected, the Hopis had a ceremony
for the death of a member of the tribe. When a Hopi
was about to die, he was placed in a sitting position
and his blanket was wrapped about him. Thus most
Hopis died sitting up. After his death his face was
painted black and a feather was placed in his mouth.
He was taken to his grave in the lowlands, still in
a sitting position. A pottery bowl of food was left by
him for four days to provide sustenance for his spirit
until it reached the Happy Hunting Ground.

Another ceremony which I saw took place in the
kiva at night. The only light in the cave was from a
small fire. As soon as the dancers had all arrived,
the fire was covered with blankets. Then I heard feet
coming down the ladder. Soon the blanket was removed from the fire and beyond it I saw a drop cur-

Tah-bo-ho-ya, Hopi, 1898.

Chief Moses.

Chief Moses, 1942.

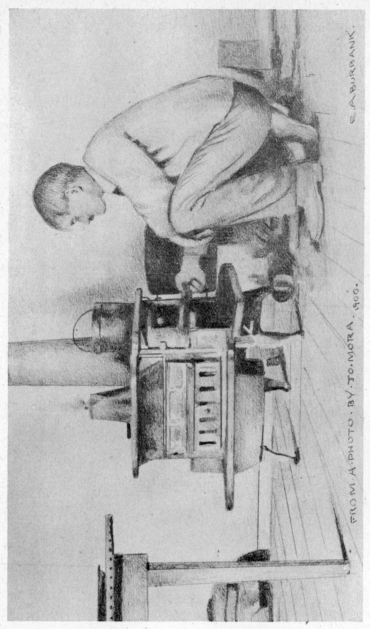

FROM A PHOTO BY JO MORA 1900.

E A BURBANK.

Copy of photograph of E. A. Burbank taken by Jo-Mora at Burbank's studio in Polacca.

tain not unlike that in a theater, only smaller. In this
curtain were two holes large enough to accommodate
a man's arm.

As the children came up, two large snakes started
to crawl from the holes. One was green and the
other black. They ran out their tongues and hissed.
It seemed quite natural that these snakes were a
man's arms covered with snake skins and that he was
holding snakes' heads in his hands.

In the dim light I made out about thirty Indians
in the kiva, all naked, their bodies tatooed like a snake
and decorated with red feathers. All wore green
masks. Among the Indians were two little boys
tatooed like their elders.

Two men stepped up and fought the snakes without much result, then the two little boys were pushed
forward within the snake's reach. The snakes
knocked the youngsters down as fast as they could
get up and finally pushed them to the other end of
the cave. While this took place, there was much
shouting and beating of drums.

One cold morning I took a walk on the mesa. My
attention was attracted by four small boys, all stark
naked. Each had a rope tied around his waist. The
other end of the rope was held by a grown Indian.
The group was accompanied by three musicians, one
of whom beat a drum while the other two chanted.

Soon they came to a house. A squaw appeared on
the deck above and poured cold water over each boy,
splashing it down from three stories up. It was
January and snow was on the ground.

When I inquired the purpose of these strange antics, the Hopis explained that this was a ceremony they indulged in once a year. They believed it caused rain or snow to come.

The Hopis had tremendous faith in their ceremonies and in their medicine men and magicians. They enjoyed exhibitions of magic, and during the intermissions in their important ceremonies they frequently turned from the sublime to the ridiculous as they watched the magicians perform their tricks.

One of these men in particular had me fooled for quite a while. After various incantations he would touch a spot on the side of a mesa and water would gush out, reminding me of the story of Aaron in the Bible. Then he would invite anyone who wished to do so to listen at the spot and hear the voice of the water spirit. Several times I listened and did hear a voice which spoke the Hopi language. Afterwards I did a little sleuthing and discovered that the magician had run a pipe up to the spot on the mesa where he brought forth the water. A confederate furnished the voice of the water spirit.

Another popular trick of the magicians was to produce a rabbit or small animal from the solid ground. I discovered that in this case the animal had previously been buried in a small cavity and was brought forth easily by removing the cover from the hole.

One day I found a group of boys having a lot of fun with a box which they had rigged up to resemble a large phonograph. As one of them turned the crank, music and talk issued forth from the box. When I looked inside I found a small Indian boy concealed in it.

The Hopis, like many other Indians, believed that the ability to draw or paint was a strong medicine possessed by the artist. They could not conceive of it as something he had studied and had worked hard to obtain. Inasmuch as I was "witch man" to them in art, they expected me to be the same in many other things. Several times my "medicine" was put to severe tests.

One day an Indian came to me and said he was in love with a certain maiden who did not seem to care for him at all. He wanted me to make medicine for him which would guaranty the girl's affection.

"That is hard to do," I told him. "I am in love with a girl, too. If I could make that sort of medicine, I would make some for myself."

I had to talk with him for hours before I could convince him that I was telling him the truth.

On another occasion, an Indian who loved to gamble at cards asked me to make him some medicine that would change the spots on the cards when he wanted them changed. I tried to show him why this was beyond the reach of my medicine, but when he left me he was still convinced that anyone who could paint pictures should be able to change the spots on a mere playing card.

AMONG THE CALIFORNIA TRIBES
THE MISSION INDIANS

With the exception of Helen Hunt Jackson, whose heart-rending story of Ramona gave us an entirely new picture of the fate of the real Americans at the hands of the white men, writers have belittled the California Indians. They have been labeled "Diggers," and have been portrayed as lazy, spiritless, dumb, and untalented.

I have painted portraits of representatives of fifty-two different tribes in California alone, and I have found them friendly and industrious, and, generally speaking, more thrifty than the Indians of many other tribes.

Once when I was painting among a tribe near Chico, one of the chiefs asked me if I knew why the white men called them "Diggers."

"Indians don't dig in the ground nearly as much as white men," he said, adding that there was no such Indian as a "Digger."

With the exception of a few tribes who lived near the wineries, I found the California Indians temperate and congenial. Near the wineries where the Indians, like Omar, had developed a taste for the jug of wine as well as bread, I had some trouble.

I recall vividly one day, when a big Indian who had been drinking wine, came to my studio swinging a large iron bar. Threatening me, he demanded fifty dollars. I watched my chance and finally wrested the bar away from him.

The next day, when he had sobered up, he came back and apologized for his conduct. Taking advantage of his mood, I persuaded him to sit for a portrait then and there, knowing that it might be difficult to overcome his objections to having his picture made. Many of the California Indians regarded photographs and portraits as very bad medicine indeed and were afraid to let me make their pictures.

My first adventures among the California Indians were on the trail of Helen Hunt Jackson's Ramona at the Pala Reservation in southern California. The natives here were known as the Warner Ranch Indians. They were members of the Agua Caliente tribe who had been evicted from their traditional homes after an extended fight which was carried to the United States Supreme Court.

The government had provided them with a three-thousand-acre reservation at Pala. One tenth of it was under irrigation. Here the Indians lived in a government-constructed village of broad streets lined with factory-built houses, all monotonously alike.

Although the Agua Caliente Indians prospered in

this modern village, the older members of the tribe were unhappy and were never reconciled to being driven from their original homes. Largely as a result of Helen Hunt Jackson's writings, these Indians were objects of great sympathy.

The owner of the Indian trading post at Pala remembered Helen Hunt Jackson and told me that he had seen her many times while she was living there working on "Ramona." With his help I was able to get an Indian boy to take me out to the house where Ramona was supposed to have lived.

The house was owned by W. B. Coots. His father had bought the Guajome Ranch on which the house stood many years before Helen Hunt Jackson came there. Mr. Coots said that he was "San Felippi" in her story.

Over the entrance of Ramona's home was a sign which read:

"Visitors tolerated but never welcomed."

Seeing this, I expected a cold reception, and was agreeably surprised when two old men who were living there received me warmly. They seemed delighted to show me around the old adobe which was built in the shape of a square. In the patio were many flowers and a fountain. The house had perhaps twenty rooms, most of them with fireplaces. The furniture was all in the old mission style.

I found the kitchen extremely interesting with its old-fashioned stove and Spanish bake oven. The inhabitants of the house still cooked by building a huge fire and heating the oven, after which the coals were raked out before the bread was put in to bake. I ate my dinner in the old dining room which was furnished just as in the Ramona days.

"The creek by the willows" of this story was all dried up, but the willows were there and the washing place too. The boy who drove me out said that he used to go swimming in the creek.

Although the chapel in the house looked like it had recently been repaired, the building and the grounds were fast going to decay, except for the typical red tile roof which apparently will last forever.

I had just re-read "Ramona" and was able to identify many historic spots about the old place. I met several old Indians who remembered both Ramona and her husband Alessandro. I even thought I had found Ramona herself when I was served by a good-natured old Indian woman who answered to that name, but she denied that she was any relation to the original.

I was able to persuade a picturesque old Indian who had been a sheepshearer in the days of Ramona, to pose for me. This old man had gone from ranch to ranch with his shears in the early days and once was the champion sheepshearer of the region.

Although the government had been generous to these Indians when they were forced off the Warner Ranch, and although they were provided with good houses equipped with running water and were given lands that were richer than those at the Warner Ranch, the natives were still homesick for their former homes.

Contact with the white men had destroyed many of their ancient customs. Still, as in the case of most of the Southwestern tribes, the women were the final authorities and they seemed to be quite capable of managing tribal affairs—including the men.

This was impressed upon me when I saw a big strapping squaw curing her husband of the drink habit. He came home drunk and in a very pugilistic mood. Without ceremony she seized him by the collar, swung him around several times until his feet left the ground, then she let go. He landed about twenty feet away. Apparently the cure was very effective, for he remained sober all the rest of the time I was at the reservation.

The natives of this region are often known as the Mission Indians. They have adopted many customs of the Spanish and Mexican people who controlled their lives for several generations. Their ceremonies are a curious combination of Spanish and Indian rites.

At Temecula the Mission Indians gave a four-day fiesta. This was a great event for them, and families gathered from an area of one hundred miles about, to participate.

Almost by magic they threw up houses of brush around a large square, in the center of which was a dancing platform. Here, for four days and nights, they presented a curious mixture of Indian war and ghost dances, horse racing, and white men's games, such as baseball and peon pelotti. They brought their food in beautiful baskets made by the squaws, and had a glorious celebration.

Five branches of the so-called Mission Indians lived in this area. Their villages consisted of comfortable houses, and they had wells and windmills to pump the water. They irrigated fertile lands and raised large crops consisting mainly of corn and hay. They raised fine horses and herds of cattle.

Practically all of these Indians were Catholics. They had great respect for their priest who lived at Pala where the mission was located.

One custom of the Mission Indians answers the criticism that they were shiftless and irresponsible. Before a Mission Indian died, he made a will in which he listed every amount he owed and all that other people owed him, even to the smallest sum. After his death, relatives administered the estate by collecting all the money due the deceased and paying all his debts.

If the amount were insufficient to meet his debts, his relatives and friends made up the difference so that he could go to the Happy Hunting Ground untrammelled by debts. If his credits were in excess of his debts, the balance went to his family.

I was told that at San Jacinto I would find the Indian woman still living who was the counterpart of Ramona. I was eager to paint a portrait of this famous Indian character and made a search for her. However, the best I could do was to find the "Aunt Ri" of the story. She was Mrs. Jordan, a little old lady, very friendly and pleasant, who lived in a large house in the village.

"Aunt Ri" told me that Helen Hunt Jackson used the lives of two Indian women to produce the character of Ramona. Both of these women were still living, she said. One lived up on the mountain at Cahuilla. She was a basket maker. The whereabouts of the other, "Aunt Ri" did not know.

I followed the Cahuilla Indians' trail up the mountain and then down to the desert. I found a number of them living near the Salton Sea. They were badly worried because the Salton Sea was rising rapidly at the time and would shortly drive them from their homes. It seemed that these Indians were doomed to be driven either by the white men or nature as relentlessly as the novel "Ramona" had pictured their fate.

The Mohaves

Among the interesting tribes of southern California with whom I lived, the Mohaves were most fascinating. They lived along the river banks near the town of Needles, cultivating their fields, and also making bows and arrows and other Indian trophies which they sold to travelers at the railroad station. The latter was their principal source of ready money.

The Mohaves were particularly fearful of having their pictures made, largely because of their belief that their bodies and all their possessions, including any likenesses of them, should be destroyed as soon as they died—so that they might go to the Happy

Hunting Grounds completely unburdened by their earthly contacts.

The strength of this superstition was impressed upon me by an incident which happened while I was among them. An unprincipled photographer had made a picture of an Indian who had died. After the Indian's death, this man made a print from the negative and placed it in a showcase. The native's widow, seeing the print, immediately bought it and burned it. The photographer made another print and placed it in the case. She bought that and burned it, too. That act was repeated several times before outraged white people residing in the neighborhood waited upon the photographer, seized the negative, and told him they would not stand for seeing the poor widow victimized in that way.

The Mohaves were tremendously interested in seeing that their journey to the hereafter was started auspiciously. I witnessed several of their death ceremonies. Preparations usually started before the Indian who was about to die had breathed his last breath.

In fact I have watched them begin by digging the oven in which they proposed to cremate him, while the dying person looked on. They would cut the wood for the fire and talk over their preparations within earshot of the dying man.

The cremation pit was dug with the longer dimension in the direction that the wind usually blew. The hole was about six feet long and four feet wide. They dug it to a depth of about two feet, with a draft shaft

at one end. Above the pit, logs were placed lengthwise to support the body. On each side logs were
piled up to a height of about four feet.

As soon as life had passed from the sick Indian's
body, it was placed, fully clothed, in a sheet and, with
an Indian at each corner, carried to the oven. Dried
grass and weeds were then placed in the pit and the
fire started.

In the meantime, the whole tribe had gathered
around, often several hundred Indians. Relatives and
friends would remove their own coats, hats, shawls,
and other clothing, casting them on the body, at the
same time wailing at the tops of their voices.

All of the deceased's possessions, including his
dogs and cats which had been killed, were placed on
the fire.

The cremation ceremonies lasted several hours.
When nothing but the ashes remained, the crowd
disappeared, leaving the widow alone to cover the
hole with sand and obliterate all earthly trace of her
husband. Then in a few days the house was burned
also, leaving the widow to make a fresh start in life.

The Mohaves were so fond of these funeral ceremonies that if an Indian did not die occasionally, they
held mock funerals and cremations for members of
the tribe who had already passed away. In this case
the ceremony was conducted with a wooden image
taking the place of the real corpse. The wooden
image had its face painted like that of the real Indian, and the lamentations were quite as loud and
sincere as in the case of a genuine death.

I encountered great difficulty in overcoming the objections of the Mohaves to having their portraits painted, largely because I could not promise that my picture would be destroyed as soon as the subject himself had passed away.

Finally I made a bargain with an old Mohave chief who sold bows and arrows to the passengers on the trains. I was to give him a quarter for every Indian whom he would persuade to pose for me. He rounded up all the models I needed, and finally agreed to sit for his own portrait. Long before I had finished the picture, he became restless and almost ran out on me.

"You no good, you take too long to make picture," he exclaimed angrily.

He could not understand why I needed more time than the photographer who had made a snapshot of him. As he started to leave the room, I headed him off and told him that if he did not sit down, I would follow him down to the train and tell all his customers that his bows and arrows were no good. He thought this over for a minute.

"All right, me sit," he said.

So I finished his picture.

THE MODOCS

Among the best of the California Indians were the Modocs, who have a bad reputation in most histories because of their uprising under their warrior chief, Captain Jack, who was hanged for his part in the insurrection.

I became well acquainted with Captain Jack's sister, whom the Modocs called "Princess Mary," and who was still in mourning for her brother. She indicated her grief by straight lines tatooed on her chin, running perpendicularly from her lower lip. From her and from two Modoc chiefs, Yellow Hammer and La-low-she-us, I learned the Modoc side of their battle with the whites.

In 1872-73, Captain Jack, with 150 braves, established themselves in a stronghold of lava and rocks, where they defied the United States Army for two years.

Yellow Hammer insisted that the Klamath Indians were the cause of the trouble. He said that the Klamaths would kill cattle belonging to the whites and blame it on the Modocs.

La-low-she-us, who was known popularly as Miller Charlie, explained that the Modocs were starving on a reservation and that the Indian agent was negligent in supplying food to them from the government. He said that Captain Jack had notified the agent that if the food were not supplied to them by a certain time, the tribe would be obliged to leave the reservation to hunt and fish for their existence. This was what happened.

The Modocs rendered such a good account of themselves in the Modoc War that they took their places in history among the great Indian warriors. Eventually about fifty of them—men, women, and children—were captured and sent to Quapaw as prisoners. At the time I visited them, there were but twelve left.

Yellow Hammer and Miller Charlie gave me an interesting account of their battles. The Modocs endured terrific hardships, and no one who listened to these chiefs could accuse the California Indians of being spiritless. I remember asking Yellow Hammer if they had good weapons.

"Yes, as good as the soldiers," he replied.

He explained that Captain Jack had accumulated the money to buy these weapons by selling skins. He had purchased and cached all the ammunition they needed.

Before the war began, Captain Jack called all the tribe together. He told them just how matters stood with the white men. He asked all who wished to fight to stand up with him. Every man, woman, and child in the tribe arose.

In view of the circumstances and of the valiant fight made by this little band of Modocs against overwhelming odds, it seems unjust that the only monument to their memory should be the scaffolding where Captain Jack was hanged.

As I have said, it was my observation that the California Indians as a whole were industrious and law-abiding. At Elk Creek I lived for a time among a band of thirty Indians who represented seven different tribes. Among them were some Kobahl-mans and Sun-pums, both flourishing tribes when the white men came to the Golden State. Of the Sun-pums only seven were left, and of the other tribe only a brother and sister were living.

In spite of its treaties with the chiefs promising lands and money to these tribes, the government had done nothing for them, and a kind-hearted rancher gave them some old lumber with which to build rough shacks on a knoll. All the money I paid to them for posing they used to buy shingles and window glass for their little houses.

At the Tejon Ranch in the Tehachapi Mountains I found a small group of Tejon Indians. Once they were lords of these mountains which later became part of an old Spanish grant, and the man who owned the ranch allowed the Indians to live there. They were industrious and did a great deal of work on the place, raising grapes, oranges, apples, and livestock, and carried on basket making.

One of the most amusing of the California Indians was an aged fellow called "Old Chief John," who lived in Hoopla Valley. He was still hale and hearty at the age of one hundred and eight. From him I learned the secret of long life.

Every day, he said, he went down to the river early in the morning—winter or summer—and dived in. After his bath, he went to a small house near by and lay down on the stone floor for a nap. His pillow was another stone. After this extra sleep he dressed and went about his day's work. He assured me that if I would do that, I would live to be a hundred.

In spite of their authority in the tribe, the California Indian women were notoriously hard workers.

They were almost beasts of burden. They were capable of prodigious feats of strength. Once on the road near Yuma I saw an Indian man and a squaw each carrying a railroad tie on their heads. In addition, the woman was carrying a papoose on her back. Suddenly the man decided he had to go back for something, so he placed the tie he was carrying on top of the woman's, and she went on with the entire load.

THE ELUSIVE PANAMINTS

I had heard of the Panamint Indians who lived next door to Death Valley. I was eager to paint them. Getting portraits of this hardy people lead to some of the most hair-raising adventures I have had while trailing Indians.

Just as I was boarding the Panamint stage at Johannesburg, a friend stepped up to me and said solemnly:

"You are going to the toughest place in America— good luck!"

When I arrived at Panamint I discovered that he was right. It was a rip-roaring mining town far out in the desert wilderness, where might was in power. At the hotel I asked the landlord if there were any Indians around. Misunderstanding my question, he replied:

"If you don't like it, you can get out of here."

I was told that there were only twelve members of the Panamint tribe still living and that they lived out in the hills. I was obliged to hang around the town waiting for an Indian to come in so that I could locate them.

The town consisted of the hotel, four saloons, one store, and a combination post office and store. The mines were several miles back in the hills. When the miners were paid off, they came to town to drink until their money and credit were used up, then returned to work.

The long hard ride out to Panamint tired me and I went to bed early. Soon I was wakened by a noisy altercation in the next room.

"Take off your clothes," someone shouted.

"I won't do it."

"Then take off your boots."

"I won't do that either."

"Take off those spurs, they'll tear the sheets."

"To hell with your sheets."

I heard heavy steps going downstairs, then coming up again. Thoroughly aroused, I looked out into the hall to see what was going on. I saw the proprietor coming up the stairs armed with a big six-shooter. Opening the door of the room next to mine, he poked the gun in and pointed it at the man lying fully dressed on the bed.

"Now you are going to take off your clothes," he said.

That was one time when the guest was not always right. He lost no time in undressing.

After a few days a Panamint Indian, whose sole name was John, came to town to do some trading. He was reluctant to pose for me because he said that several members of his tribe who had posed for a photograph had died. However, he did come to my room and let me make a sketch of him, and he pointed out a place near the top of the mountains where he said I would find the rest of the tribe. It was a peak about five miles away.

The only way to get out there was by stage. The stage driver, who was a graduate of Yale, was the toughest man in town. He had such a bad reputation that the other citizens of Panamint refused to let him carry a gun. On the way out, he regaled me with stories of his adventures around Death Valley. He said that while he was prospecting in Death Valley he ran out of water. When he was about dead from thirst, the Indians found him and nursed him back to health.

I was amazed at the skill with which a man drove a twenty-horse team up the mountains loaded with materials for the miners. His horses were attached to a wagon in pairs, one on each side of a long chain. The road was narrow and winding. When they came to a sharp turn, it was necessary for the horses on one side to jump the chain. As each horse came to the sharp point in the road, the driver would call out to him by name.

"Jump over, Tom."

Each horse jumped as his name was called. Most of the horses would be pulling on the outside of the chain when the curve was rounded.

Near the top of the mountain which Chief John had pointed out, I found quarters with a ranger. I set out to find the Indians and finally located a few white tents where they lived. I found John and another old Indian there, but when I approached the encampment the squaws screamed and ran away as fast as they could. I couldn't get close enough to them to buy a basket. John explained that they were afraid I would take their picture and that they would die.

The ranger with whom I was staying told me that two Panamint Indian women had married white men and lived in Darwin, a mining town twenty miles away. He thought I could get them to pose.

I journeyed over to Darwin and located these two women one Sunday morning. They were playing cards with a group of other women. As soon as they saw me, they screamed and ran as had their sisters up on the mountain, so I never did get a portrait of a Panamint Indian woman.

Darwin had once been a prosperous mining town, but when I arrived there it was rapidly becoming what it is now—a ghost town. One man owned the hotel, the store, the blacksmith shop, and the bus line, not to mention the saloon which was attached to the store. Everyone called him Charlie.

Charlie was sick, and although confined to his bed, he continued to manage all of his enterprises. His bed was within calling distance of all of his commercial operations. Customers walked in and served themselves. After telling Charlie what they were taking, they called out "Charge it, Charlie," and from under the bed clothes came his answer, "All

right, folks." I think I was the one customer he had
who did not ask him to "Charge it."

Riding back with the Yale man, I listened to an
account of a trial he had witnessed in Darwin in its
heyday. An important case was being tried in the
courtroom when a drunken miner stumbled into the
chambers.

"What in hell is going on here," he demanded.

The judge rapped for order.

"Bailiff, arrest that man for contempt of court."

Arrest sobered the intruder so that he apologized
for his rude interruption of justice.

"I invite you all to come over and have a drink on
me," he announced.

Whereupon the court adjourned and witnesses,
jurors, the judge, and the prisoner moved in a body
to the saloon to participate.

CHAPTER SIX

THE WARRIOR SIOUX

Because of their savage victory over the whites in the Custer Massacre, the Sioux had the reputation of being "bad Indians," hostile and treacherous. I found them anything but that when I visited them seeking to paint the portraits of their great chiefs. I was particularly interested in Red Cloud, Rain-in-the-Face, and other chiefs famed in the wars which represented the last stand of the Indians on the Prairies.

The Sioux called themselves "the Dakotas." They were the strongest confederation of Indians in the country, judged by man power. As the westward movement of the white people pushed the Indian tribes of the Mississippi Valley before it, the Sioux confederation assimilated these tribes as they were driven from their native lands.

All of the tribes in the Sioux confederation had a grudge against the white man, naturally. They resisted with all of their might the whites' invasion of the prairies. As the Sioux nations themselves were pushed farther and farther west, they in turn drove their traditional enemies, the Crows, before them, until the latter took their stand in the heart of the Rockies.

One of the greatest of the Sioux chiefs was Red Cloud. He was a "good Indian," meaning a chief who had held his tribe in line and had abided by the treaties made with the white men, even though the whites themselves consistently disregarded the treaties. Red Cloud had made numerous trips to Washington to see the Great White Father on behalf of the Sioux.

The government had built a two-story house for Red Cloud. I visited him and told him that I would pay him if he would pose for his portrait. He stalled me off, saying that he wanted to see what the other Indians thought about it before he agreed to pose. Though I called on him frequently for several months, it was always the same story.

Finally one day I encountered Red Cloud walking with Chief Spotted Elk, who spoke English well. Using Spotted Elk as an interpreter, I addressed Red Cloud.

"Tell Red Cloud I am coming out to his house tomorrow to paint his picture," I said. "Tell him I want him to be ready for me. My things are too heavy to carry all that way for nothing."

On the following day I went out wondering whether or not my trip would be successful. Somewhat to my surprise I found Red Cloud waiting for me in his attic, all dressed up in his fine feathers and ready to pose.

Red Cloud turned out to be a fine model. While I was painting his picture he asked Spotted Elk to tell him how it was getting along. Spotted Elk told Red Cloud that I was making his eyes look as though he could see a long distance.

"I am glad," said Red Cloud. "My friends can see me as I looked when I could see."

This was the first intimation I had that he was nearly blind.

Red Cloud was so pleased with the things his friends said about the first portrait of him that he came down to my studio later on his own account and posed for another picture, this time wearing his gorgeous yellow-beaded jacket.

Although Red Cloud was a good model he always took too much time out to rest. I would have to hunt him up. Usually I would find him in the store haranguing the other Sioux and denouncing the Crows. He had had many battles with the Crows and regarded them as his bitterest enemies.

I discovered that at Red Cloud's home his wife was the boss. Any time the Indian agent or officials wanted something of Red Cloud, they went to his wife. Had I known this I might have secured his portrait much sooner.

Rain-in-the-Face was one of the most famous of the Sioux, having been one of the leaders in the Custer battle. I was eager to paint his picture—until I saw him.

I had asked several Indians to let me know when Rain-in-the-Face came to town. I was eating my

Chief Red Cloud, Sioux, 1899.

Chief Flat Iron, Sioux, 1899.

Chief Sitting Bull, Sioux, 1875.

Chief Blue Horse, Sioux, 1898.

dinner one evening when an Indian told me that Rain-in-the-Face was in the store. Hurriedly dropping my knife and fork, I went over to see him. They pointed out a stolid looking Indian with a round German face, dressed in a policeman's uniform.

He was about five feet four inches tall. Having been crippled in the Custer fight, he went about on two crutches. I was so disappointed when I saw him that I did not speak to him and went back to finish my dinner.

Later on I reconsidered and decided to paint his portrait anyway. By that time he had departed for a gathering of the Sioux at a point about forty miles away. A friendly Sioux and French half-breed offered to take me there.

Arriving the next morning, I found Rain-in-the-Face eating breakfast with some Indian women. Studying his face, I realized that perhaps he did have qualities I had overlooked. A squaw man whom I knew invited Rain-in-the-Face over to meet me. Shortly, the famous Sioux rode over on his horse. Through an interpreter I told him about my work and asked if I might paint his portrait.

"How much you pay me?" asked Rain-in-the-Face.

"Two dollars for six hours," I said.

He readily accepted the offer. However, when I tried to get him to take off his policeman's uniform and put on his Sioux war custome, he stoutly refused. He pointed to the hundreds of Indians gathered about on the plain.

"You will not find even an eagle feather among them," he told me through the interpreter.

This was the truth. Few of them had any Indian clothes left. So I painted the great Rain-in-the-Face in a blue policeman's uniform.

For a studio we used an old abandoned log jail. Rain-in-the-Face was a good sitter but he would pose for only one picture. He was a very sober Indian and would not laugh at the jokes of the other Indians nor have much conversation with them.

When the squaw man who had acted as interpreter for us left, I asked him how to say, "It is time to rest," in Sioux. Presently I used the words on Rain-in-the-Face. He looked at me for a moment in astonishment and then went outside and rolled around on the ground laughing. Whatever it was the squaw man told me to say, Rain-in-the-Face found it very funny indeed.

An old man clerking in the Indian trading store at Fort Yates told me about an encounter Rain-in-the-Face once had with Tom Custer, who was General Custer's brother. One day when Rain-in-the-Face was in the store, Tom Custer came in and arrested him. As he departed this old clerk said he heard Rain-in-the-Face say in Sioux:

"The first chance I get I will cut out your heart and eat it."

General Custer's brother died with him in the massacre, and the story was that Rain-in-the-Face made good his threat.

After the "Wounded Knee" fight, the Fort Yates

Sioux abandoned their Indian costumes as they fled. The clothing was given to the Pine Ridge Indians. Yellow Bird, a canny Sioux, had traded until he owned practically all of the Indian costumes on that part of the reservation. From his fine collection I was able to help fit many a chief in true war regalia.

I was interested to observe how the Sioux fastened eagle feathers to their hair. They bored small holes through the quill and made small braids of their hair which were threaded through the holes. Thus the feathers looked as though they belonged to the chief's head.

Chief Kicking Bear was one of the most perfectly built Indians I have ever seen. When he was in Washington the Smithsonian Institute had a model made of his body as representative of the finest physique in the Indian race.

After I had painted his portrait, Kicking Bear took a great liking to me, and urged me to come and live with him, an offer which I had to refuse.

He had several children and was tremendously fond of them. All of the Indian children on the reservation were required to attend school. One time Kicking Bear's offspring became slightly ill—not seriously so, but enough to keep them home. The authorities thought they were playing hooky and sent a policeman to bring them to school. Kicking Bear refused to let them go.

When the policeman returned the second time he found Kicking Bear standing guard on his porch with a gun in his hand. The incident was reported to the Indian agent but he, being a sensible man, let the matter drop.

The Indian youngsters, particularly the boys—being true creatures of the wild—resented school. Chief Stinking Bear's son disliked the classroom so much that when he was forced to attend he shot himself. It was hard for the Indians to accustom themselves to confinement.

Stinking Bear was a noted chief with a keen sense of humor. The portrait I painted of him was one of the most popular pictures I have ever made. One day while he was posing in my studio a little Indian girl came into the room.

"My papoose," said Stinking Bear. "Hungry. Give her money."

I gave the little girl a quarter.

The next day another papoose came in and Stinking Bear made a similar plea. It cost me another quarter. On the third day there was still another papoose. We repeated the ceremony.

I was curious to see how far he would carry it, so I contributed a quarter each day until the sixth, when I told him that if he had any more children, to bring them in at once so that I could get the charity over with. Stinking Bear saw that the game was up.

"No more," he said.

Sioux humor was at its best in the course of a dance given by the tribes at a large ranchhouse near Pine Ridge. I had been invited to this dance and a pestiferous tourist who was stopping there asked the Sioux if he might come with me. He promised to bring tobacco for everybody if he were invited. The Sioux had refused him an invitation at first but on the promise of tobacco they told him he could come.

The dance was held in a large hall. They built a fire in the center of it. Around this fire they danced almost naked, their bodies painted in gaudy colors. Shortly after we arrived they discovered that the tourist had not brought the tobacco as he had promised.

The Sioux decided to give him a good scare. First they tied him to a stake, then piled wood all around him, meanwhile telling him that they were going to burn him at the stake. I have never seen a more pathetic figure than this man begging for his life. They finally released him and he hot-footed it to the store to bring the promised tobacco, never doubting for a moment but that the demonstration was real.

While the Indians were posing for me at my studio, I paid for their meals at the hotel. First they thought that one serving of meat, potatoes, coffee, and bread was all that they could have. Later on they learned that an American Plan dinner meant all they wished to eat, whereupon they started in to do a real job of eating. The proprietor of the hotel became alarmed. He asked me to put a limit on their eating.

"You can't fill up an Indian," he said.

One day while I was painting a Sioux' portrait, two white women dropped in. Evidently they had not seen each other for some time and immediately began an incessant chatter which they kept up for some time. When they left, the Sioux turned to me. He made a motion with his hands which in sign language means "talk."

"White woman yappa, yappa, yappa."

The great national hero among the Sioux was Sitting Bull who led his people in their last stand against the white men. Everywhere I went I heard stories of Sitting Bull.

Although he was a ferocious fighter, Sitting Bull used to love to visit the school where his children were receiving the white man's education. The teacher had a special chair placed for him so that he could sit and listen to the students reciting their lessons. He attended classes day after day with the younger generation.

Sitting Bull was the leader of the Ghost Dance, the mysterious ceremony which gained great influence among the Indians, causing much unrest. It was a dance to prepare for the end of the world which the Indians believed to be imminent.

It was the Sioux' belief that great clouds of dust would come and cover the earth, killing off the white men and their families. The Indians and their children would be saved and their hunting grounds would be returned to them. The Ghost Dance was in the nature of a ceremonial prayer to speed the day.

This dance, plus the Indian belief, lead to great unrest on the reservation. The authorities became concerned, and finally the teacher in whose classes Sitting Bull used to love to sit, decided to speak to him. He asked Sitting Bull to use his power to curb the dance, adding that it was untrue that the white man's world would end.

"It will only make trouble for the Indians," he said to Sitting Bull.

The great Sioux chief looked at him, then made this reply,

"Long time ago white people believed much water would come down and drown all the bad people."

The situation finely became so serious that the government agent decided to act. He sent two policemen, both Sioux Indians, to arrest Sitting Bull. They found Sitting Bull taking a nap. He consented to go with them without making trouble.

In the meantime other Indians, learning of his arrest, had gathered in large numbers on the nearby hills. One of these Indians shot a policeman. The other policeman, thinking it was Sitting Bull who had killed his partner, shot Sitting Bull.

Buffalo Bill Cody, who was Sitting Bull's friend, had been sent by the government to try to induce the old chief to stop the Ghost Dance. He was only a few miles away when he heard of Sitting Bull's death. Buffalo Bill turned back satisfied that with Sitting Bull's death the Ghost Dance would end. It did.

I visited Sitting Bull's grave at Fort Yates. However, I learned later that the Indians had exhumed his body and buried it in another place known only to themselves. The spot was a Sioux shrine hallowed by the memory of their great leader.

Chief Little Wound was said to have more influence over the Sioux than any other living Indian.

His father had been killed by Chief Red Cloud. Both Little Wound and Red Cloud sat for me in the same room, though at different times, of course.

Little Wound posed for me in full war dress, wearing a silver medal given to him by President Grant, and his portrait attracted great attention. He was held in great esteem by the white people who considered him a dependable Indian, and at the same time he was much beloved by his own people.

One day I went in to Yellow Bird's store at Pine Ridge and discovered the place crowded with Indians crying and wailing and wringing their hands. They told me that Little Wound was dead. He had gone to Omaha and, getting off the white man's street car, he had fallen backwards striking his head on the pavement.

One of the most colorful of the Sioux Indians was Red Jacket, who accompanied Buffalo Bill's circus to Europe. In London the Indians were presented to Queen Victoria who attended the show. The Queen complimented Red Jacket on his wonderful hair.

While I was living among the Sioux I discovered an old white man who had been captured by the Indians when he was about ten years old, while his family was crossing the plains in a prairie schooner. The Indians had killed all of the party but him and they had treated him always as one of their own. After living eighty years with the Sioux, this man resembled them in looks as well as in manners. He was as Indian as a man could be except for color.

This white Sioux told me that the Indians had

rigid laws for hunting. They never killed buffalo or deer during the calving season. When on the hunt, they killed only enough game for food and never wasted it. It was not until many years later, when the white men had practically exterminated the wild life of the country, that the states began to make similar laws.

"You see that barn over there?" he said. "I have seen it filled with buffalo robes that the traders bought for a cup of sugar apiece."

Two of my good friends at Pine Ridge were Elmer Little Chief and his wife. They were educated Indians and both taught school. Every Friday evening they came to town bringing their little three-year-old daughter and her dog. They were very pious Indians. I noticed that on Sunday morning all three of them went to church regularly.

Every time the little girl would see me, she would say to her mother,

"Many Brushes calls me 'Little Sweetheart.'"

One Sunday morning as they were going to church, I said to the little Indian girl,

"Let your father and mother go to church and you stay outside with me."

She drew down my head and whispered in my ear.

"I will go with papa and mama," she said, "and the doggie can stay with you."

So I had the pleasure of the dog's company that Sunday morning.

Elmer Little Chief was four years old at the time of the Custer Battle. He said that the Sioux were camped at the mouth of the Little Big Horn, and he could remember that a great many Indians were in the river bathing themselves and their horses when General Custer and his troops rode up, shooting as they came.

Elmer Little Chief was helping his mother erect their tepee and she had sent him up to the top to tie the thongs to the pole, so he had a good view of the shooting as he looked across the river. After a few minutes, he said, everything was confusion as the Indians rushed into their tepees preparing for the fight.

One day a circus came to town. Elmer Little Chief and his wife took their daughter to see the animals. Afterwards Mrs. Little Chief came to me. She was very angry.

"What do you think," she exclaimed. "One of the circus men wanted to buy my daughter and asked how much I would sell her for. As if I would not think as much of my daughter as a white woman would of hers."

The little girl was with her father one day when he met Chief Stinking Bear. They shook hands. The little Indian girl looked up at her father.

"Now, father, you go and wash your hands," she said in Sioux, then added in English, "after shaking hands with that dirty Indian."

Everybody laughed but Stinking Bear. Walking over to the little girl, he shook his finger at her.

"It is not right that you should tell him to wash

his hands," he rebuked her. "You are an Indian as well as your father and I."

Indian superstition almost got me into serious difficulties when I was painting Iron Crow. He posed for me in his war colors, wearing his imposing crown of feathers, but when I had finished his head and was about to start on his body, he had to go away to be gone for some time. Since I could not wait for him to return, I had another Sioux pose for his body.

Iron Crow was sure something terrible would happen to him because his head was painted onto another Indian's body, and a good many of the devout Sioux shared his views.

Chief Flat Iron had travelled to Europe with Buffalo Bill's Wild West Show. He loved to tell about that trip across the ocean. Buffalo Bill chartered a boat to carry the whole circus. It was a very slow craft.

Everything was all right for the first few days of good weather, but when a storm became so severe it was necessary to lock everyone below decks, the Indians believed they were going around in a circle and getting nowhere. Flat Iron almost made me seasick illustrating with his hands how the ship rolled.

Finally, he said, they held a council and decided that the captain did not "savvy ship." They sent for him. When he arrived they asked if he knew where they were. The captain said he did. He showed them their position on the map. That, of course, meant nothing to the Indians.

"How soon we see land?" they asked him.

"Eight days," replied the captain.

The Indians were skeptical but they decided to count the days. Sure enough, in eight days they sighted land. After that they could not say enough for the captain.

"Heap savvy ship," said Flat Iron.

I was eager to get the Indians' account of the Custer Massacre. An old man clerking at the trading post at Fort Yates had heard the story from many of the survivors who lived around the reservation.

Just before the Custer Battle the buffalo, deer, and other game on which the Indians subsisted had become thinned out in that vicinity. The Sioux were largely dependent upon the rations issued by the government. A new Indian agent had been appointed. He looked over the reservation and asked why the Indians were not at work.

This man evidently was unaware of the Indian superstition about the land. They believed that all things were planted by the Great Spirit for his children. They said it was flying in the face of Providence to plow up the soil and plant other things than what the Great Spirit grew.

The white people in the vicinity also tried to explain to the agent that the soil there was not suitable for cultivation and that it was a cattle and sheep country. He scoffed at the idea and said if the Indians would not work he would cut their rations in two.

The Sioux called a conference to which they invited the new agent and all the white people in the neighborhood. They chose Chief Gaul, one of their finest orators, to speak.

Very eloquently Chief Gaul outlined their belief that the Great Spirit would be offended if the ground were disturbed. He said that if the Indians were allowed to go out and hunt, they could provide for themselves without aid from the Great White Father, but that if they were confined to a small area, the Great White Father would have to give them food or they would starve. He concluded by warning the agent that if their rations were cut the Indians would be obliged to return to their old hunting grounds in the Little Big Horn where they still could hunt buffalo, deer, and other game.

The agent was stubborn and unsympathetic. He cut the rations and soon the Sioux were on their way to the hunting grounds where they joined up with the Cheyennes and other independent tribes. It is a matter of record that the famous battle which took place on the Little Big Horn was brought about when General Custer and his troops were sent to bring the Sioux back to their reservation.

One of the chiefs with whom I became very friendly was No Flesh, who was a veteran of the Custer battle. I asked him to tell me what he had seen. He agreed to tell me if I would come over that evening to his tepee where his son could act as an interpreter.

When I arrived at No Flesh's tepee, his wife hospitably placed a sheepskin outside the door for me to sit on. No Flesh started his story by drawing a map on the ground with a stick. He had just finished putting in the location of the Indians and the soldiers and was pointing out where General Custer stood, when his wife came out.

"Don't talk any more," she told No Flesh. "If you do, white man will not like you any more."

In spite of my protest that his story would make no difference in my attitude toward him, No Flesh obeyed his wife. He would talk no more. As a compromise he agreed that I might paint his daughter's portrait. Her name was "She-Comes-Out-First."

No Flesh sold me a beautiful pair of moccasins that his daughter had made for him. When she heard that I had bought them, she felt very badly and asked to see them. She examined them and gave them back to me. Later she got even with me by charging me thirteen dollars for some Indian trinkets which a trader told me later were worth only two or three dollars.

The costume worn by She-Comes-Out-First was an amazing bit of finery. It was largely beads and weighed forty pounds. The dress tired the girl so much while she was posing that her mother took turns sitting in her place, toward the end.

One day while I was among the Sioux, the men of the tribe fell to joshing a squaw ninety years old, telling her she was too old, that she could not dance. This ired the old woman, and she put on an impromptu dance as lively as any of them, in spite of her years.

Blue Wing, an attractive young squaw, wanted to

pose for me, but she had no Indian costume. So I painted her in a calico dress.

One of my best friends among the Sioux was Chief Blue Horse. He had lost one of his eyes while chopping wood. He was quite old but he rode in each day on his horse to pose.

Blue Horse had a droll wit and was always ready with a joke. One day he entered the trading post while they were unwrapping some bacon. He told us that when he died he didn't want to be doubled up like the bacon but would like to be put in a box long enough so that he could stretch out.

He came into my studio one day and said, "You paint four pictures of me." When I asked him why it should be four, he said, "Because I say so."

Blue Horse had a wonderful war bonnet and other Indian clothes to match it. He was a fine old Indian and I was glad to agree to paint four portraits of him.

While I was working on the first one he told me that his daughter was very ill and asked me to go home with him that evening. I found the girl lying on a pile of blankets dying of consumption.

I did what I could for her and proposed getting a doctor the next day, but in the morning Blue Horse rode in and said that his daughter had died during the night. As soon as the body was buried, Blue Horse had the house torn down. He told me that he would go to a place one hundred miles distant to visit with some other Indians and forget his troubles.

He asked me to lend him seven dollars, saying he

wanted to buy calico for one of his daughter's good friends. I told him he was too poor to buy calico for other people.

"Look here, my friend," said Blue Horse, "I want that calico to give to my daughter's friend so that my daughter will be happier in heaven."

So I gave him the money.

"In one moon I return," he said.

With his thumb and forefinger he made a circle to indicate the sun. He pointed to the position of the sun at nine o'clock in the morning.

Blue Horse returned exactly when he said he would and found me painting the portrait of another Sioux. The old chief pointed his finger at me accusingly.

"You lie," he said.

I asked him why.

"You promised to finish my picture when I came back."

I explained that I could not wait for him but that as soon as I had finished the portrait I was working on I would resume his picture. This satisfied him.

One day while I was painting Blue Horse an old white man came in and gave him some money. The white man turned to me.

"Let me tell you why I am good to this old Indian," he said. "About twenty-five years ago several of us were prospecting for gold not far from here. A band of Sioux captured us. They were planning to burn us at the stake when Blue Horse heard about it, and he rode forty miles to tell them that if they burned

Rain-in-the-Face, Sioux, 1898.

White Swan, Crow, 1899.

Chief Gray Hair, Crow, 1897.

Curley, Crow, 1897. General Custer's scout in the battle at the
Little Big Horn River.

us he would burn every one of them. They released us unharmed."

Blue Horse came into my studio one hot day, fanning himself with a big turkey wing. He sat down on my bed and, not noticing, put his hand down on a sheet of sticky fly paper I had placed there. To pull it loose, he grabbed the other end of the fly paper with his other hand, and soon was tangled up gloriously. Before I could come to his rescue, he had managed to stick the fly paper on his little dog's back. In no time at all, the pup had dashed around the room, attaching himself to first one object, then another. The situation was funny to everybody but Blue Horse.

"Bad medicine," he said in disgust.

After that first loan of seven dollars to Blue Horse, our financial dealings became very involved. Occasionally he would borrow a dollar and now and then he would pay one back. I kept the account on a piece of paper. Blue Horse kept his account in his head. One day I asked him how we stood.

"Me owe you two dollars," he said.

"No," I replied, "you owe only one."

We had quite an argument about it and finally went over to see Yellow Bird who owned the store and spoke good English. With Yellow Bird's help I finally convinced Blue Horse that he owed me one dollar instead of two, but it looked for a time as if the issue were going to be the end of a beautiful friendship.

After I left the Sioux reservation I received a

letter from Blue Horse. He had dictated it to a friend and mailed it to me. It is one of the finest things I have ever received. It read as follows:

"I raise my pipe above my head and say, Great Spirit I pray Thee to be good to my friend, the son of the shadow maker. Toward the pine trees, North, cold wind treat him kindly, toward the rising sun, East, great sun shine on his lodge each morning, toward the place where the shadow maker lives, South, bless your son, toward the land of the setting sun, West, saying waft on the breezes our friend this way, and, lowering my pipe of peace, I say, Kind Mother Earth, when you receive my friend into your bosom, hold him kindly. Let the howl of the coyote, the roaring of the bears and mountain lions, the cold blast of the wind, swaying the tops of the pine trees, be a sweet lullaby to him, that shaketh the hand of your friend, Blue Horse."

CHAPTER SEVEN

THE WHITE MAN'S FRIENDS— THE CROWS

The Crows were the traditional friends of the white men, and I was surprised when I invaded their reservation, that none of them would pose for me, no matter what inducements I held out.

Hugh Campbell, the Indian trader with whom I was stopping, offered to make an investigation and find out what was the matter. After he had talked to them he came back to my room laughing.

"They say that when you get back to Chicago you put poison on their pictures and that the Indians who posed for them drop dead."

I was astounded at this superstition, the strangest one I had ever encountered. Campbell said that he would call the Indians together and try to get the idea out of their heads. I was present at the pow-wow.

"Haven't I always been your friend?" he asked them.

"Yes," spoke up a Crow chief, "you have always been our friend."

"Did I ever lie to you?" asked the trader.

"No," declared the chief, "you never lied to us."

Then the trader told them that it was not true that I put poison on their pictures. He asked them to pose for me, and from that time on I had no difficulty.

We found that the "poisoned picture" story had been started by Chief Pretty Eagle. He was one of the head chiefs and was a fine man. After the meeting, he was the first Crow to pose for me.

Once more he was almost my undoing. After I had painted his portrait he promised to bring in his youngest daughter to pose. When she failed to come in, I rode out to their house two miles away to see what was the matter. I found Chief Pretty Eagle lying under a tree, sick.

"You no good, you bad medicine," he told me accusingly. "Me pose for picture, now heap sick. No can paint my little girl."

Upon inquiring I found that Pretty Eagle had gotten his feet wet and had contracted a bad cold which he blamed on my portrait painting.

It was not until some time later when Pretty Eagle went away to an Indian dance that I was able to get his daughter, whose name was "All-Hers," to pose for me at the Crow Agency before he could prevent the picture. All-Hers was the belle of the Crow reservation and Pretty Eagle was proud of her.

One day I met Pretty Eagle down at the agency. I asked him what brought him there. Pretty Eagle had some difficulty in expressing himself in English, so in answer to my question he danced a few steps.

That meant he was going to attend the great dance about to be held.

I watched him go down the road. He soon met another man who evidently asked him the same question, because Pretty Eagle performed the same steps. Then a little girl greeted him, with the same result. As far down the road as I could see him Pretty Eagle, who was well-known and popular, was giving his occasional dance. If these demonstrations tired him in any way he showed no signs of it at the dance that evening. He danced straight through until sunrise.

Pretty Eagle was a fine Indian, highly respected by everyone for his courage. Once when the railroad was seeking a right of way to build their line across the reservation, they sent representatives to purchase the right of way. The Crows called a council at which a railroad man presented the necessary papers for signature. One of the Crow chiefs rose, drew a six-shooter, and said he would kill the first Indian that signed the papers. Without hesitation Pretty Eagle stepped up, asked for the papers, and signed them, with his back turned to the discontented chief. The other chiefs followed his example.

My studio, when I was working on Pretty Eagle's portrait, was Hugh Campbell's residence. Mrs. Campbell was away. So we worked in the living room. Mrs. Campbell had many beautiful satin and silk sofa pillows. When it came time for him to rest, Pretty Eagle would arrange the pillows in a big pile and lie among them. In a few minutes he would be sleeping as soundly as a child. All I could see, when I went to awaken him, would be his eagle feather. I have often wondered what Mrs. Campbell would have done to us, had she returned to find Pretty Eagle buried in her lovely pillows.

When the railroad built the roadbed across the reservation, it bumped into a shack in which an old Crow squaw lived. The hut stood squarely in the right of way. To the overtures of the officials who offered to buy the shack and move it, the old woman turned a deaf ear.

Finally a white man who understood his Indians offered to buy the shack for two hundred dollars. The offer was accepted. First he turned the money into silver dollars. Calling on the old squaw, he showed her a handful of the "cartwheels" and asked her if she were willing to sell her house. She indicated that she was. He asked her to hold out her skirt. When she did so, he threw about twenty-five dollars into it, and stopped.

"More," said the old squaw. He tossed in ten more silver dollars.

"More," she repeated. He kept on tossing dollars into her apron until he had thrown about fifty.

"Stop," she said.

That was all he paid for the property—the balance being "velvet" for him.

One of the most beautiful sights I ever saw was a great Crow Indian war dance held one Fourth of July. Several hundred Indians took part in this dance. Some of them were nude, wearing only breech clouts, others were decked out in gay Indian finery.

The bodies of the braves were painted in a most gorgeous manner. Those who wore garments were resplendent in designs of barbaric taste. All of the dancing braves wore feathers, furs, beads, and bones.

Each brave adopted his own color scheme and each was consistent and harmonious with the rest of the dancers. The Crows surely have a fine sense of color and remarkable skill in working out their designs. None of them seemed to have too much decoration— just enough to be in keeping with the general scheme.

Even the onlookers dressed in picturesque costumes. The squaws and children were all painted. Their dresses were decorated with elk teeth, beads, and porcupine quills. Many of them wore beautiful deer hides decorated with patterns of which any designer might be proud.

Some of the Crows attended the dance on horseback, their horses having eagle feathers fastened to their tails. The saddles suggested those used in olden times by the Spaniards, but were painted and decorated with beads. The bridles, too, were profusely ornamented.

The mania for decoration extended even to the dogs, each one having some ornament to do him proud.

Throughout the dance there would be intermissions every hour to rest. During that time the squaws would pass around large bowls of dog soup, a delicacy which caused the Crows to smack their lips and pass their dishes back for more. I was obliged to refuse it, having seen how the soup was prepared.

Two squaws would hold the dog on its back, stretching out its legs. Another would take a stick and roll it back and forth across the dog's neck, choking it to death. In this way they lost none of the blood. The dog was then dropped into a kettle of hot water to loosen the hair. After the hair was removed, the dog was cut up and put into another kettle to boil.

The war dance was attended by a number of Sioux, who were the traditional enemies of the Crows. The Sioux were a very important part of one feature of the ceremony. At intermissions in the dancing one or another of the Crow chiefs would stand and point his finger at a Sioux.

"I killed his father in battle," he would say.

Whereupon the Sioux would make reply,

"It is true, but in a later fight I killed his father."

Then another Crow would arise and make a similar claim which would be refuted by a Sioux.

This barbaric Crow war dance was the most colorful scene I ever experienced in all my years among the real Americans. I was the only white man present, and many times I have thought back over the experience and wondered if it were but a dream.

One of the Crow chiefs whose portrait I painted had a small owl trained to perch on his head. All during the war dance this bird fluttered about, occasionally resting on his master's head and remaining there while he danced.

I painted the Crow with the owl on his head. After I had finished painting the owl and the top of the owner's head, I did not need the bird any more, so I put it outside. But every time the door opened, the owl fluttered in and insisted upon resuming his position on the Indian's head.

An Indian is a splendid model for a certain kind of photographic portrait. He sits still uncomplainingly and seldom moves a muscle. However, he challenges an artist's artistic sense by sitting bolt upright after the manner of the wooden Indians in front of cigar stores. He wants every hair on his head to be in perfect position. Some of my subjects would even dip their hands in sugar and water and rub it through their hair to make it stand erect.

How different these same Indians when they were not posing! I really enjoyed having the Indians with me and nearly always had one or two eat with me. During the meals they were jolly and full of fun. They loved to tell stories, although their sense of humor was frequently tinged with cruelty.

One of the Indians who frequently ate with me at the Crow reservation was half Sioux and half Cheyenne. The full-blooded Crows loved to tease him about his mongrel ancestry.

While I was there, William Jennings Bryan crossed the reservation during his presidential campaign. I accompanied several Crows down to the railroad station to see him. The Great Commoner spoke from the rear platform of his car to the assembled Indians and whites. It seemed to me that there was little interest in what he said, and so I was astonished when we got back to the reservation to see the Indians telling one another in sign language what had taken place.

First they put one hand over the eyes like a visor of a cap—that meant "white man." Then they put one hand over the head waving it back and forth like a war bonnet—that meant "white man chief." Next they struck one hand on the other like a blacksmith pounding an anvil—that meant iron. Finally they waved their fingers in the air indicating smoke from the stack of the locomotive. Evidently Bryan had impressed them as being a big chief.

Most white people assume that the Indians smear their war paint on indiscriminately, but the truth is that each daub has a significance, as does each feather an Indian wears.

White Swan, for instance, wore three feathers in his hair. That denoted the number of wounds he had received in the Custer fight. Fifty years later in the World War the white men learned to do the same thing with wound stripes.

White Swan also wore red stripes of paint around his arm, indicating the number of Sioux he had killed, and yellow ones for the Cheyennes.

The Crow chief Karnys, wore white marks on his forehead to indicate his potency as a medicine man, and red marks on his shirt to show the number of horses he had stolen from the Sioux.

Chief Medicine Crow was one of the most remarkable of the Indian artists. On one occasion he made a trip to Washington, D. C. While there he visited the museum. On his return to the reservation he painted from memory pictures of practically all of the mounted animals he saw in the museum. His drawings were surprisingly accurate.

Chief Bear Claw was the great story teller among the Crows. Nearly every day I would see him surrounded by young Crows who listened to his funny stories. At the conclusion of a story they would roll all over the ground laughing, but when I tried to get him to tell me some of the stories, he always refused.

One day a white man asked Bear Claw if he had ever noticed that so many white men were bald. Bear Claw had noticed it, he said, and had wondered why it was so. The white man jokingly replied that it was because the white man told so many lies. He said that every time a white man lied he lost a hair. Bear Claw passed this on for the truth and the story did not enhance the white man's reputation among the Indians.

One day a Crow saw a white man riding a bicycle. It was the first one he had ever seen.

"White man heap lazy," he said. "Sit down to walk."

The government decided to build an ice plant out on the reservation. When the Indians were told that the building was to house ice-making machinery, they scoffed at the idea, saying that only the Great Spirit could make ice.

Eventually the plant was completed and the Indians were invited to inspect it one day when the thermometer stood at one hundred in the shade. Each Indian was given a piece of ice. They held the ice in their hands, tasted it, and finally became convinced that it was really ice. They were awe-stricken.

"White man heap smart," they said. "Great Spirit makes ice only in winter. White man makes it in summer."

One of the most interesting Indians I met anywhere was Chief Plenty Coups. He was a Nez Perce by birth but had been stolen by the Crows when he was a baby. He grew up to be an influential Crow chief, a great rival of Pretty Eagle. He was down on the government rolls as a Crow.

Plenty Coups' name was derived from the French word indicating a coup, or touch. Having been a great warrior in his day, Plenty Coups had made plenty of coups.

I was eager to make a portrait of this popular chief. He asked me how long it would take to paint his picture. I told him "Four sleeps"—meaning four days. Plenty Coups replied firmly, "No, too long. Two sleeps." He added that after two sleeps he would have to go to a dance and I must paint him in two days or not at all. I finished him in two days, but had to work at top speed to do it.

For an Indian he was quite wealthy and when he came to my studio he brought with him his valet, his squaw, and a large mirror. He was the proudest Indian I ever saw and reminded me of a peacock, when he donned his magnificent regalia. Even with the assistance of his valet it took him nearly an hour to get ready to pose.

Plenty Coups spent a long time getting his face decorated just right. When my patience had become about exhausted, he sat down in the chair and told his valet to hold the mirror so he could take a final look at himself. One feather in his hair did not suit him. He straightened it. Finally his valet assured him that everything was right.

"Go ahead and paint," said Plenty Coups.

The wily old chief stationed the valet beside me to keep him posted on the progress of the painting. Frequently he would ask what part I was working on. If I happened to be painting his arm, Plenty Coups would pull all the wrinkles out of his sleeve, to my great annoyance. Finally the picture was finished and I allowed Plenty Coups to look at it.

"Heap good," he said, adding that if I would come to his home at Prior Creek he would pose for another portrait.

When I rode out to his home, on the stage—a distance of seventy-five miles—a forest fire was raging near by. Plenty Coups said he was sorry I had come so far but that he would have to go help fight the forest fire. I waited several days for them to get the fire under control, but finally had to return without seeing Plenty Coups again.

The old chief was a merchant of no mean ability. He owned a store at Prior Creek where he, his squaw, and one other Indian did a thriving business.

Plenty Coups' squaw was his third wife. The old

chief had two wives when he came to the reservation. He was sincerely attached to both of them, but the government told him he would have to give one of them up. Plenty Coups passed through a trying period of indecision but finally conformed to the white man's dictates.

However, to everyone's surprise he kept the wife who was sick with consumption, letting his healthy squaw go. For years he supported them separately and the discarded woman took no other husband. When the sick wife became bedridden, the cast-off squaw returned to be her nurse until her death.

Everyone rejoiced that the separated ones would be reunited, but Plenty Coups, without ado, took himself a new wife and the other one went back to live by herself.

Plenty Coups' ability to cipher was about equal to that of a six-year-old boy. Hence, keeping his accounts straight was something of a problem. The merchant chief designed a bookkeeping system which was unique. When a customer paid cash, Plenty Coups dropped the money in the box and the transaction was over, but for the accommodation of those who did not have cash he kept books.

On a sheet of common brown wrapping paper he drew a picture of the customer or the customer's name. There was no misreading the sketch which indicated Yellow Bird, Mrs. Many Shells, or any other customer. No bookkeeper's ledger could have been so plain.

Blue Moccasin was painted green because Plenty

Coups had no blue paint, but Yellow Jacket and Red Fox were in the right colors. In Iron Thunder's picture there was a strong resemblance to that of "Knows-how-to-go-to-War," but the difference in headdress is significant to an Indian.

"White man" was indicated by a hat, coat, and tie. "Black white man," which meant Negro, wore the same kind of dress. Short Bear suggested the old custom of cutting off a dog's tail behind his ears, because the whole length of his body was cut off. "She-Sees-among-Plenty" was represented as standing amidst a number of other Indians. Big Nose was just what his name indicated. Child-in-the-Mouth was shown as devouring a small creature with its arms outspread and fingers straight.

When Mrs. Many Shells came in and paid five dollars on account, Plenty Coups erased the figure at the top of the picture and substituted for it the new figure showing the total due. When accounts were paid in full, Plenty Coups drew a wiggly line through them. At the end of the year all accounts were squared and the sheet of brown wrapping paper was burned.

I asked Plenty Coups for some of the old account sheets. The wily merchant sold them to me for twenty-five cents apiece, and they are now in the Ethnological Department of the Field Columbian Museum in Chicago.

I have said that Plenty Coups was proud as a peacock. The object of which he was proudest was not his war costume but his timepiece.

A white man, P. B. Weare, grazed some cattle on land belonging to Plenty Coups. Mr. Weare had no hair on his head, so the Crows called him "Bald Eagle." In payment for the use of Plenty Coups' land the white man gave the Indian a gold watch bearing the inscription, "From Bald Eagle to Plenty Coups." After receiving the watch, the old chief walked with the majesty of a king.

Inasmuch as the Crows had been the allies of the whites in the Custer Battle, I thought that I might get some of them who had been in the fight to tell me the Indian version of it.

Custer's scout at the time of the battle was Curley, a Crow, whom I found living in a tepee with his wife and son. The government was digging an irrigating ditch there, and Curley was working with his team of horses on the project. I introduced myself to him and asked him if he would pose for me. He ask me how much I would pay him. I told him $2.00 for six hours. He said, "No, I get $3.50 a day from the government, with my team of horses." I told him I did not want to paint the horses. But he replied, "There's no use arguing about it. You pay me $3.50 a day and finish the picture in one day, as I am leaving here this evening to go home with my family." I agreed, but told him he would get no rest until the picture was finished.

That evening I invited Curley and his family to have dinner with me at the boarding house. They were ready to talk on almost any subject until I

Chief Plenty Coups' store account. Being unable to read or write, he kept his records by means of rude drawings. The numeral is what the Indian owes.

1. White man; 2. Sits-on-the-Fence; 3. Big Eyes; 4. Colored Man; 5. Hairy Moccasin; 6. Knife; 7. Elk; 8. Worm; 9. Dog; 10. Sees-Among-Plenty; 11. Holds-the-Enemy; 12. Yellow Bird; 13. Long Hair; 14. Big Nose; 15. Medicine Girl; 16. Yellow Woman; 17. Sees-the-Enemy; 18. Little Deer; 19. Coyote; 20. Plenty Coups; 21. Three Strikes; 22. No Face; 23. War Club; 24. Walks Pretty; 25. Black Bird; 26. Big Moccasin; 27. Red Man; 28. Long Hair; 29. Lone Wolf; 30. Big Head; 31. White Hair; 32. White Horse.

Chief Burnt-All-Over, Southern Cheyenne, 1899.

Chief Two Moons, Northern Cheyenne, 1898.

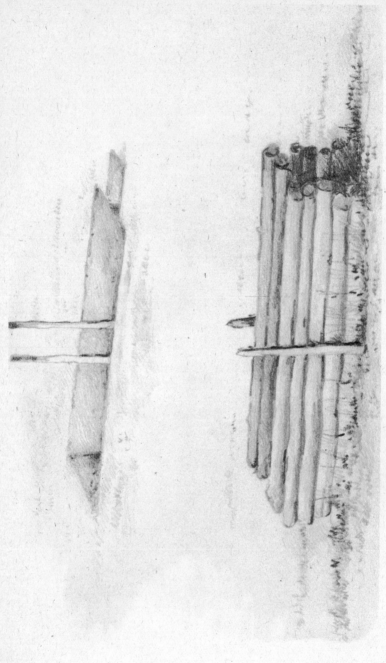

Mojave cremation pit and stack of fuel for cremation.

mentioned the Custer fight. Immediately Curley became dumb.

My best Indian account of the fight was from White Swan, another Crow, who had been a scout for Reno. After I had painted his portrait, White Swan agreed to show me over the battlefield. He was deaf and dumb, the affliction having been caused by the blow of a Sioux who had struck him over the head with a war club during a battle. So White Swan had to tell me about the Custer fight in the sign language and by drawing rude pictures illustrating features of the battle.

One of the sketches showed a soldier trying to desert. White Swan explained in the sign language that Reno had sent him after this man. The sketch showed White Swan killing the soldier by striking him over the head. I came to the conclusion that he was bragging about his part in the Custer fight.

One day while White Swan was posing, an old Crow named Gray Hair—the last of the medicine men—came into the studio carrying a bag of herbs and stones. From his bag he took a stone and rubbed it over the hearts of all of the Indians present, then rubbed it over my heart. When I inquired what it was all about, the Indians told me that it was a sure cure for a bad heart.

Gray Hair had his long medicine pipe with him. He filled it with tobacco, lighted it, and pointed it toward the north, muttering a prayer. Then he pointed it to the east and to the west. Finally, just as he was pointing the pipe to the south, he tipped over too far in his chair and went backwards sprawling on the floor.

It was so funny that I burst out laughing. Not an Indian in the place cracked a smile, however, out of respect for the medicine man. White Swan went outside to have his laugh.

On the site of the Custer battlefield there was a hotel run by Fred Server. Several times he dropped into my room in the evening to talk. From him I learned the Indian story of the fight just as he had heard it from the Crows.

Server said that he was present when Custer and Terry held their memorable conference before the fight. He heard Custer tell Terry that he would start with his troop and go to the mouth of the Little Big Horn and that Terry was to follow the next day.

Server was with Terry's troop and at one point where they crossed Custer's trail they saw a man coming on horseback, riding fast. For a time they could not make out whether it was an Indian or a white man. When the rider came closer they found it was Curley, the Custer scout. He was tremendously excited.

Curley told Terry that Custer and all of his men had been killed. Terry refused to believe Curley and sent him to the rear. Terry decided to make camp inasmuch as they were not to meet Custer until the next day.

The next morning, shortly after they had started out, they met Reno and his troop. When Reno heard Curley's story about Custer and his men, he replied that on the day before he had heard heavy firing off in the direction of the Little Big Horn.

The combined troops set out immediately to look for Custer and his men. Six miles away they found them—all dead. Custer, with many of his men, lay in one group.

Server said that all of the dead soldiers had their feet and lower limbs full of bullet holes. He thought this occurred because the Indians were going around the group in circles shooting low so as not to shoot their own warriors on the opposite side.

He said also that Tom Custer's heart had been cut out and a knife run through it. He claimed that this had been done by Rain-in-the-Face, a Sioux, who had licked the blood from the knife in fulfillment of his savage vow.

MY CHEYENNE CHALLENGE

One day while I was painting the portrait of White Bull, the Cheyenne, another Indian came into the room waving a tomahawk threateningly. He was chattering in an Indian tongue, and I asked Dave Big Man, who was an interpreter, what the newcomer was saying to White Bull.

"Put this painter out of the room," he translated. "Your life will go with the picture. Don't sit for him." Dave Big Man added that the Indian was Chief Little Chief, the orator of the Cheyennes and a great friend of General Miles.

The tomahawk that Little Chief was waving had twelve notches, each one denoting a soldier he had killed.

After he had departed I asked where Little Chief lived, and next day I set out for his tepee which was about two miles from the studio. I found only his wife and children at home and did the best I could to make friends with them by giving them candy, money, and tobacco.

Shortly Chief Little Chief returned. He was very hostile and asked, with a scowl, why I was there. Then noting that his wife and children were happily occupied with the candy, his attitude changed at once.

Diving into his tepee he returned with a large pocketbook filled with old letters, much soiled from handling. I read them all and made comments on them. Most of them were written by prominent people, including General Miles who concluded one letter with, "Be good to this old Indian."

I spent an hour or so with Little Chief and his family but said nothing about painting his portrait. They were all cordial when I shook hands with them and left.

Early next morning, to my great surprise, Little Chief came into my studio ready to pose for his portrait.

Little Chief was a good model but an inveterate cigarette smoker. I thought I would try to smoke him out, so I hired another Indian to roll a good-sized pile of cigarettes and hand Little Chief a fresh one as rapidly as he finished the one he was smoking.

Little Chief puffed steadily without pause until he had consumed ten cigarettes. Then he said suddenly, "No more." After that he smoked no more while posing for me.

Little Chief was a natural orator and story teller. While he was posing, Indians would come into the studio to listen to his stories of the feats of the Cheyennes when he was a boy. One day his audience seemed especially interested in what he was saying.

My curiosity got the better of me and I asked Dave Big Man what Little Chief was talking about.

Dave Big Man hesitated to tell me, saying he did not want to repeat the things Little Chief was saying. I persisted and finally he explained that Little Chief was telling the other Indians that he wanted to die killing a white man. He wanted it to be a fight to the death for both of them.

Being young and foolish, I decided to have some fun with the old Cheyenne chief. I turned to Dave Big Man.

"Tell Little Chief that I want to die that way myself," I said.

Little Chief looked at me in surprise.

"Why do you want to die?" he asked, puzzled.

I told Dave Big Man to tell him that I was many hundreds of miles away from my family, that I had seen many hard times, that often I slept in barns, box cars, or depots, with only my overcoat for a cover. I said that I wanted to fight Chief Little Chief because he had told the other Indians that I was bad medicine and that they should not pose for me.

"I don't want to fight you," Little Chief replied through the interpreter. "You are kind to us. You pay us well for sitting for our pictures. You have been kind to my wife and children."

I listened attentively and then told Dave Big Man to explain that I was in earnest but that I did not want to fight with old-fashioned weapons like the bow and arrow or tomahawk but preferred to shoot it out with revolvers at a distance of ten feet. I suggested that in this way we both would be sure to be slain.

When I finished with my bravado speech I rose from my stool, put away my palette and brushes, and removed my coat. I said that I was ready.

Little Chief and the other Indians were astounded. "No," he said, "I will not fight you."

If he had accepted my challenge I think every hair on my head would have turned white right there.

The news spread like wildfire over the reservation. My studio was soon filled with young Cheyennes who wanted to see the white artist who wanted to fight Little Chief with six-shooters.

"Many Brushes is a brave man," they said.

They little knew that I was shaking in my boots. But after that I enjoyed special status among the Cheyennes.

One of the finest looking Indians I have ever seen was the Cheyenne chief, American Horse. I was eager to paint his portrait and went out to visit him one Sunday forenoon. I found him taking a sweat bath.

The Western Indians had great faith in these sweat baths and made use of them for many ailments. They used the baths to invigorate themselves when they became fatigued. Even while on the trail an Indian would occasionally pause to take one of these baths.

Chief American Horse first built for himself, from willow poles and skins, a tepee so small that there was barely room for him to crawl inside. It was really a toy tepee. Once inside he removed his clothes and sat on a block of wood.

While he was thus engaged, his wife was heating several stones until they were almost white-hot. These she rolled into the tepee near him. American Horse then poured water on the hot stones, causing them to give off clouds of steam which completely filled the tepee. I doubt if the most modern Turkish bath could have provided a better steam treatment.

My curiosity to know more about the steam bath annoyed American Horse. He asked me if I wanted a bath, and said that if I did not wish one to please go away immediately, which I did.

Later American Horse posed for me. He was a proud Indian deeply conscious of his dignity, and made a fine portrait.

When I painted White Wolf, who was not a chief, American Horse heard of it. He came into the studio and said to me angrily, "You told me that you only painted chiefs."

I explained that he was mistaken, that I painted principally chiefs but also other Indians if they were interesting.

"White Wolf no chief," he kept repeating.

I could not make him understand my point of view and so, to soothe his dignity, I finally gave him a dollar to settle the argument and get rid of him.

Wolf Robe, the Cheyenne, was one of the most arrogant Indians I ever encountered. He could look right at you without deigning to see you. He accepted cigars with stolid indifference from anyone who tried to make friends with him. The only intimation he gave that he would like another, when the cigar was gone, was the wistful look he gave the butt when he placed it in a conspicuous place on the floor.

He tried to conceal his interest in his surroundings, but when he was alone in the studio I caught him examining his portrait with keen interest. Upon hearing approaching footsteps, he would resume his haughty demeanor.

Wolf Robe knew that he was a valuable subject and demanded three dollars a day for posing. Inasmuch as he was the perfect type of American Indian, I paid it. His face carefully painted, his head bedecked with feathers, and bearing his red sandstone pipe, he would stride into the studio with the air of a king, seat himself, his eye fixed on a mark on the wall, and remain as immovable as a bronze statue until I put aside the palette.

Unlike most Indians, Wolf Robe was always well supplied with money. He invariably carried a pocketful of bills and small change. I used to pay him with large bills purposely to see if he could make change. He always could.

About the most widely published picture I ever made was of Medicine Woman, a Cheyenne squaw. She always came into the studio with her father who painted her face as she should appear when dancing. Her beautiful leather dress was ornamented with more than one hundred elk teeth.

Medicine Woman was one of the best dancers among the Cheyennes. On the reservation they had

built a large round house in which they held their
war dances, usually at night. The men danced nearly
naked, always wearing war paint and occasionally
decorating themselves with eagle feathers.

Most of my subjects were reserved, but occasionally I found an Indian who was jovial and talkative.
Chief Burnt-All-Over was one of the latter. He had
a long and honorable record as a warrior and his face
was crisscrossed and zigzagged with lines in every
conceivable direction.

I was curious to know how he happened to be
named Burnt-All-Over. He said that once when he
was a little boy his mother was cooking soup in a
large iron kettle suspended by a chain from a pole
over the fire. In a mischievous moment he turned
the kettle on the chain, twisting it as far as it would
go, then let go. The kettle spun around throwing
the scalding hot soup all over him. Hence his name.

One day Burnt-All-Over and I were discussing the
technique of scalping. He said that sometimes the
victor took only the scalp lock, at other times the
whole scalp. His demonstrations of the operation
sent the shivers down my spine.

First he showed how the knife was drawn around
the scalp, how the vanquished warrior was placed on
the ground, and how the victor put his foot on the
shoulder of his enemy, seized the hair with both hands
and jerked the scalp from the head. As he reached
the finale, Burnt-All-Over added a touch of realism
with a cryptic "Plook."

While I was working on his portrait, Burnt-All-

Over had lunch with me as my guest at a restaurant. One day he asked me if I would give him the twenty-five cents I ordinarily paid for his luncheon, if he did not eat anything.

I agreed on condition that he stay there with me and be ready to pose as soon as I had finished eating. That was agreeable to him. So each day thereafter he ate no lunch, took the quarter, and saved it.

When we finished his portraits, he bade me an affectionate good-by, holding my hand in both of his. I wondered when I would again see my good friend, Burnt-All-Over.

A short time later I took cold. After a day or two I managed to resume my painting. One day, as I was sitting at my work with my back to the door, I heard someone approaching. I knew it was an Indian by the sound of his moccasins. I turned and saw first a feather, then the red face of Burnt-All-Over.

"I heard my friend, Many Brushes, was sick," he said. "I got on my horse and rode forty miles with Indian medicine for him. I am glad to see he is painting."

My Indian friend's devotion touched me deeply.

"You stay here with me," I said. "Seven sleeps, seven breakfasts, seven lunches, seven suppers here with me. In the evenings we will smoke. All the smokes you want."

Burnt-All-Over was delighted. He stayed with me, and posed for another portrait.

A young Cheyenne who had killed a white sheep-herder, was wanted by the U. S. troops patrolling the reservation. He sent word that he wanted to die for his crime, but he wanted to die fighting. He promised to appear on his horse in his war paint at a certain hour on a hill he designated. The soldiers could shoot him, but he would try to kill as many of them as possible before they got him.

True to his word, he appeared at the designated hour. The Indian agent was surrounded by troops, and two sheriffs with their deputies were present. Two thousand Indians in blankets were gathered there, too, and under his blanket each Indian carried a rifle.

The sheriffs wanted to arrest the boy, but the Indian agent, sensing the situation, held them in check.

"If you make a move, everyone of us will soon be dead," he said.

The daring young Cheyenne sat on his horse for a few minutes. Suddenly he wheeled and galloped off, making his escape. Not a shot was fired.

The refugee hid in a near-by swamp and defied the white men's efforts to catch him. Finally, old Chief Two Moons, to whose tribe the young Indian belonged, agreed to bring him in, to end the tense and dangerous situation. The boy was tried and sent to prison. In seven years he died. I was told that seven years was as long as any Indian could stand confinement.

While I was painting Two Moons' portrait, George Bird Grinnell, the famous Indian authority, had a room next to mine. He was making records of Indian songs and speeches. Two Moons did not know what

Grinnell was doing. One day the voice of an Indian boomed from the next room.

"American Horse is in there," exclaimed Two Moons.

He went into the next room to greet American Horse, but could not find him. American Horse's voice was coming out of the horn of the phonograph. Poor old Two Moons was flabbergasted, to put it mildly. His one idea was to get out of there in a hurry. It took the combined efforts of Grinnell, Dave Big Man, the interpreter, and me, to hold him until we could make him understand this strange medicine.

A good many Cheyennes had participated in the Custer Battle, and I knew Two Moons was one of them. One after another I asked them to give me the Indian story of the fight. Two Moons was the only Cheyenne who would agree to tell me all about it. I waited breathlessly for his story. It was brief and to the point.

"Heap big fight. Heap dust," he said. But no more.

Chief Moses lived at a place called Moses Coulee, which had been named for this famous old Cheyenne chief. He was a privileged character on the reservation. For services rendered the government, he was granted one thousand dollars a year pension. He spent this money for fine horses and fur clothing.

When I asked him to pose for me, he said, as usual, "How much?"

I offered him two dollars a day and he asked for three. When I agreed to three he raised it to four, then five, and finally six, at which point I decided to leave him unpainted.

I happened to have with me a portrait of Chief Joseph, the Nez Perce. Chief Moses looked at it and then at me.

"You would never have painted that picture if Joseph had not surrendered just when he did," he said.

"Why?" I asked him.

"I had a bead on his heart," said Chief Moses.

MY GREATEST INDIAN

The greatest Indian I have ever known was Chief Joseph, the Nez Perce—a soldier, statesman, and gentleman by any standard, civilized or savage. In many ways he was the most remarkable man the Indian race produced.

I had admired Chief Joseph for the masterly way he handled his people during the retreat from their hunting grounds in Idaho in 1877. I was eager to paint a portrait of him before he passed on to his reward.

The early French traders named these unusual Indians the Nez Perce because of the peculiar way they pierced their noses and wore nose rings. The Nez Perces welcomed the Lewis and Clark party and, after that contact with the white man, the tribe sent an embassy to St. Louis in search of "The Book of the Great White Spirit." The Nez Perces not only accepted Christianity but they practiced it, and few white men have lived up to its creed as did Chief Joseph when he became chief of the tribe.

The Nez Perces, in a series of treaties, ceded much of their hunting grounds to the white men on the advice of Chief Joseph, and contrary to the wishes of older counselors of the tribe. Chief Joseph agreed to stay on the reservation allotted by the government. Unfortunately in 1877 gold was discovered on the Nez Perce lands, a rush followed, and Lewiston, the first capital of Idaho, was hastily thrown up in the midst of the Indian reservation.

The young braves regarded this as a breach of treaty rights, which it certainly was. Chief Joseph urged patience and peace, but the younger men revolted, and several white men were killed. Once hostilities had broken out, Chief Joseph realized that the white men would demand vengeance upon his tribe. The only safety to the Nez Perces lay in flight, and Chief Joseph set out with his tribe for Canada.

Encumbered by women and children and their possessions, he led the Nez Perces from the Wallowa Valley in eastern Oregon across Idaho, through the wilderness of the Yellowstone, fighting several battles with pursuing troops of the United States Army, until he was within thirty miles of his goal. There, almost at the gateway of freedom, Chief Joseph and his tribe were trapped by General Miles.

General Miles' admiration was stirred by the strategy and gallant generalship of Chief Joseph. He urged Chief Joseph to surrender to avoid further bloodshed. Joseph agreed to do so on the promise that their lands would be returned to the Indians—

Chief Joseph, Nez Perce, 1899.

Memorial to Chief Joseph.

Hawgone, Kiowa, 1897.

Gi-aum-e Hon-o-me-tah, Belle of the Kiowas, 1898.

a promise which General Miles made in good faith, but which the United States Government failed to carry out.

On the occasion of Chief Joseph's surrender, October 5, 1877, he made a speech that left few dry eyes among the troops who heard it.

"I am tired of fighting," said Joseph. "Our chiefs are killed. Looking Glass is dead. The old men are dead. It is cold and we have no blankets. It is the young men who say 'yes' and 'no.' He who led the young men is dead. The little children are freezing to death. I want to look for my children and see how many of them I can find. Perhaps I shall find them all among the dead. Hear me, chiefs. I am tired. My heart is sick and sad. From where the sun now stands I shall fight no more forever."

In his biography General Miles said that if Chief Joseph could have studied at West Point, he would have been a great American general.

Chief Joseph made several trips to Washington on behalf of his people and other Indians. Wherever he appeared, the great Nez Perce by his dignity and earnestness created a profound impression. I had heard of him from many sources and looked forward to meeting him.

Chief Joseph lived in Nes Pilen, Washington. The trip involved a long train ride over a branch line from Spokane to Wilbur, where I hired a rig and drove forty miles to the Columbia River. Here my rig turned back and an Indian ferried me across the river in a dugout canoe. From that point I rode on horseback, accompanied by an Indian guide.

The first man I met at Nes Pilen was the blacksmith. He approached me, looking me over critically.

"Partner," he said, "where do you come from?"

I satisfied his curiosity by telling him how far I had come to meet Chief Joseph and paint his portrait. The blacksmith took me to the agency and introduced me to the Indian agent. The latter told me that Chief Joseph lived about three miles distant in a small wooden house built for him by the government. He told me about Chief Joseph's two wives and finally sent word to Joseph asking him to come in and see me.

When Chief Joseph came in his broad-brimmed felt hat he reminded me very much of a Quaker. He was an imposing Indian, gentle, dignified, serious. After we had visited awhile, I broached my mission of painting his portrait. Unlike all other Indians I have painted, he did not ask how much I would pay. Instead, he asked for twenty-four hours in which to think over the matter. The very next day he returned and agreed to pose.

Chief Joseph wanted to be alone while I painted his portrait, so we arranged to use the office of the reservation doctor. I had asked him to paint his face as the Nez Perce warriors did when preparing for battle. I always carried in my kit some ordinary dry paints—black and white and other colors such as the Indians used—so that lack of paint could not be used as an excuse for not wearing the proper colors.

Some Indians use paint on nearly every part of their body. The common practice was to lay the dry paint on their tongue, moisten it, and then use a narrow stick to transfer it to their bodies or their hair. Sometimes the Indians mixed the paint with water and smeared it on their faces with their fingers. Among certain tribes, when a warrior had engaged in a hand to hand combat with an enemy, he would dip his hand in the red paint and place it on his chest, carrying the print of the red hand into battle.

Because it took an Indian an hour or so to paint himself in the morning, I always insisted that the sitter come an hour early so as to be painted and ready for posing at nine o'clock. This was necessary to get in a full six-hour day of painting.

Among the Nez Perces it was the custom to paint little red dots on their faces. Chief Joseph accomplished this by dipping a small round stick in the paint and applying it to his forehead and cheeks. I also carried in my kit several eagle feathers in case the model had none to dress his hair. Joseph painted the white part of the feathers yellow, as was the Nez Perce custom.

I always placed my canvas between myself and the sitter. The Indian could see by the back of the canvas what part of his body I was painting. He would invariably hold his pose well until the head was finished, then relax.

Most of my subjects sat stiff and silent while posing, but Chief Joseph conversed with me all the

time I was working on his portrait. His favorite
subject of conversation was General Miles whom the
great Indian admired tremendously. The General
reciprocated this admiration. Chief Joseph also liked
to talk about the good things he had eaten, particularly back in Washington where he had visited
General Miles.

"Oysters hi-you-skookum," said Joseph.

I enjoyed working with him so much that after
finishing the first portrait, I asked Chief Joseph to
sit for another.

"No, one is enough," he said, although he did
promise to pose for me again if I would come back
some other time.

The government had built a very comfortable
little house for Joseph and I think he was satisfied
there although he was separated from his tribe. He
had several trunks containing his Indian clothes and
other relics. Some of these he had not opened for
years. He agreed to open them to show me his things,
but found that he had lost his key. The blacksmith
had to break the trunk open for him. Joseph had
collected many beautiful things including expensive
furs. From one of the trunks he presented me with
a rare Nes Pilen basket.

While I was there, Joseph and I hunted prairie
chicken several times. During these trips he told me
a number of stories. He said that his real name in the
Nez Perce language, Hin-mah-toe-yah-ley-klickt,
meant "Distant rumbling on the mountains." It was

amusing to hear him imitate this rumbling in his deep voice.

Joseph told me about an army officer who had come to Nes Pilen with his son who was not well and the father wanted him to live an outdoor life. He asked Joseph to take care of the boy and finally left the youngster with the Indian.

One of Joseph's wives made a small tepee for the boy to sleep in. Joseph himself made bows and arrows and taught the youngster to use them. He gave the boy a pony to ride. For two years Joseph and the youngster were together most of the time, fishing, hunting, and roughing it.

By that time the boy had learned the Indian language and spoke like a native. The father sent money to pay the boy's fare back to civilization. The youngster refused to go. Then the father sent an officer to get the boy. Again he refused to go, saying that if he returned to the city he would soon be sick again.

Joseph, although he had become very fond of the white lad, remained neutral. Eventually the father made the long trip to Nes Pilen himself and took the boy home by force. Joseph chuckled as he told me how this white boy had preferred his adopted Indian father to his real father.

The Nez Perce Indians were an exception among all the Indians I saw in that they treated their animals kindly. Most Indian tribes would work their horses unmercifully, but the Nez Perces were extremely careful and kind to them.

Joseph had a fine team and when I left Nes Pilen

he arranged to take me to Wilbur where I could get
the train. En route, Joseph stopped every child we
met—either white or Indian—and talked with them.

We talked a great deal about the country through
which we passed. Pointing to a tree, Joseph would
say, "You see that one stick—all the time good
water." By that he meant there was a spring near
by.

He told me how his father had called him to his
deathbed and said, "O Joseph, never sell the land in
which your father's and mother's bones are buried."

Joseph had promised his father never to give up
the Nez Perce lands. He said that later though when
the whites were after the land so hard, it seemed
wiser to give them up and start for Canada than
fight the white men.

Arriving at Wilbur, we induced the cook at the
hotel to prepare us a supper, although it was late.
We enjoyed this and afterward sat smoking our
cigars until bedtime, like two old partners.

The next morning, after I had insisted upon paying him for bringing me to Wilbur, Joseph asked me
to accompany him while he did some shopping. He
had a large list of supplies to buy. At the butcher
shop the butcher started to cut off a few pounds of
beef, but Joseph said:

"No, I want all." He bought the whole hind
quarter.

When I bade him good-by, he said, "You come back
and I will pose for two more pictures."

It was two years before I returned to Joseph's

Chief Black Coyote, Arapahoe, 1899.

E. A. BURBANK.
NEW HAVEN
MICH.

Chief Pokagon, Potawatami, 1898.

home. I arrived at Wilbur on Sunday morning and strolled out to a place where several Indians were camping around a fire. Among them I found one of Joseph's wives. She told me that he was in Idaho with his people but would be back in a few days.

I was busy painting other Indians when he arrived at Nes Pilen. Shaking hands, he said, "I cannot sit for my picture now because several of our tribe have died and we must have a ceremony.

Joseph invited me to this ceremony. It was simple and impressive and so different from the typical Indian ceremony that it seemed almost civilized. The tribe gathered in a large tepee where all washed their hands in the same basin, after which Joseph prayed for the souls of those who had died. I could not help but contrast it with the savage ceremonies of the Mohaves when members of their tribe passed away.

Chief Joseph was a very religious man but he objected strenuously when Missionaries asked to be allowed to build a church on the reservation.

"No," he said, "you white men have too many gods, we Indians have but one god." What he meant was that the white men had too many churches of different denominations.

Joseph promised to visit me the next time he made a trip to see the Great White Father. On my return home I wrote him a letter asking him when he thought he could come, but before he could have received it I read in the newspapers that Joseph had passed away.

"Chief Joseph died of a broken heart," the doctor at Nes Pilen said. What he meant was revealed at the great Indian chief's grave. I felt that I had lost a true friend, that our country had lost a great man, and that the finest gentleman among all the real Americans had passed to his final reward.

THE COMANCHES AND KIOWAS

Bone-e-tah, the Comanche, was the dude of the reservation when I arrived at Fort Sill, Oklahoma, to spend several weeks getting the portraits of both Comanches and Kiowas. In frontier days these two plains tribes combined to wage long and bitter warfare against the Spaniards who pushed from Mexico and Texas into their hunting grounds.

Being eager to paint a Comanche in full war regalia, I borrowed an elaborate costume from the doctor at the reservation. Bone-e-tah loved to dress up, but there was one obstacle to wearing this costume—it had been worn by a dead man. The original owner died while wearing it.

They say every man has his price, and Bone-e-tah's price was $1.50 extra a day for wearing this regalia. My regular fee at Fort Sill was $2.00 a day. Bone-e-tah charged me $3.50.

This was almost my undoing. Indians have a strong sense of justice and when the others heard that I was paying Bone-e-tah more than they were receiving, they called a council one night in one of their tepees.

When I arrived I found Haw-gone, the Kiowa, presiding. As is invariably the case among Indians, they brought up the issue fairly and without anger.

"Is it true," asked Haw-gone, "that you pay Bone-e-tah more than you pay the other Indians?"

"It is true," I replied.

"You must pay the others the same as you pay Bone-e-tah," he decreed.

"All right," I agreed, "I will pay them the same if they will consent to wear the costume that has been worn by a dead Indian."

That put an immediate end to the incipient strike. The rest of the Indians agreed to continue on the original terms.

Haw-gone, the Kiowa, a tall powerfully built Indian, was an excellent artist whose work compared favorably with that of Naiche, the Apache. His favorite subjects were horses, Indians, and wild turkeys, and he painted them in full color.

Haw-gone would sit and watch me day after day as I worked, studying my technique. I taught him all that I could about painting and, upon my return to Chicago, sent him a full set of water colors. The big Indian loved to dabble with his paints and was an attentive student. His work showed marked improvement after the few lessons I gave him. Some of his pictures were reproduced and others were accepted for the Newbury Library in Chicago. If Haw-gone had been able to secure real art training

in his youth, I have no doubt he would have become
an artist of note.

As a rule, Indians have no eye for proportions,
and as a consequence in depicting men, horses, buffalo, and other subjects, they make rather grotesque
caricatures rather than accurate likenesses. Haw-
gone was an exception to this rule, for he drew very
true to scale, except in one case where he drew six
fingers on a hand instead of the regular five which
nature provides. He made several pictures in colors
for me and could draw and paint a turkey very ac-
curately. One of his pictures was reproduced in a
Chicago magazine.

Gi-aum-e Hon-o-me-tah, who was the niece of
Haw-gone, was one of the loveliest Indian girls I
have ever seen. Her home was at Rainy Mountain,
but she was at Fort Sill a great deal and was the
belle of the reservation. Her father was a Kiowa
chief and Gi-aum-e was treated like a little Indian
princess.

She was smart as well as beautiful and spoke English well. She was clever, likewise, with the sign
language. Her sweetheart, E-ah-ti, lived in a village
seventy-five miles away. He often rode over on his
horse to see her. One day I asked her if E-ah-ti did
not think that she was the nicest little Indian girl on
the reservation. She did not answer me, but when
outside where I could not see her, she put her hand
through the doorway and replied in the sign language, "Yes."

Gi-aum-e was very bashful and when she first

started to pose for me, she sat for a week without saying a word. When she finally did become acquainted, she became quite talkative. She and her friend, another Kiowa girl named Ton-had-ile I-c-o, who always accompanied her, sang Kiowa songs to me, after which they translated them into English. All of the songs were of a religious nature.

"Ton-had-ile" means "lame" in Kiowa. Ton-had-ile I-c-o was quite lame. The two girls were very close pals and were always together.

I had in my studio a lay figure which I brought out to the reservation to use in painting the Indian costumes after the Indians themselves had become tired posing for their portraits. The two little Kiowa girls had great fun with that figure. They loved to paint its face like a Kiowa and dance around it, laughing heartily at the artificial Indian.

Once when the circus came to town, I invited Gi-aum-e to go with me to see the show. She seemed to enjoy it tremendously until a clown came out before us and in a very pathetic mood told a sad story. This made Gi-aum-e cry. She was a very tender-hearted youngster and felt very badly when grown people scolded mischievous youngsters.

The circus brought to town the first elephant the Indians on that reservation had ever seen, and they were quite flabbergasted at its appearance. They would not go near it, nor would they even consider it as an animal, insisting that it was made of India rubber.

Once when the officers at Fort Sill gave a dance, I

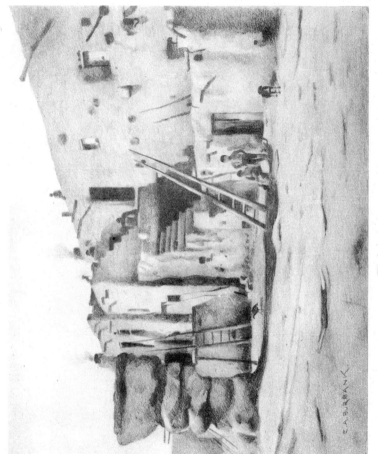

Walpi, Arizona.

Walpi Trail.

asked them if I might bring Gi-aum-e and her friend. Everyone was very fond of both girls and they were glad to invite them. The two Indian girls enjoyed the party but were very much astonished at what took place. Once I caught them together in a corner laughing and I asked them what it was all about. They explained naively that they were laughing because they thought it so funny for one girl to dance with so many different men. They also felt that this was very improper.

Gi-aum-e's mother enjoyed dressing her daughter up in very beautiful Indian clothes. Among the Kiowas the girls pull out their eyebrows and paint the part in their hair either red or yellow. They are fond of colors and trim their clothes with elk teeth, white horsehair dyed different colors, and beads. If Gi-aum-e could have received a good education, she would have been a very bright woman indeed.

I corresponded with her for some time after leaving Fort Sill. Finally one letter remained unanswered. When I returned to Fort Sill I inquired about her and was shocked to learn that she had died suddenly.

The Kiowas had a keen sense of humor and loved to talk about visitors in the sign language. When I first arrived among them I wore a mustache and whiskers, as was fashionable among well-dressed men at the time. When I caught the Kiowas describing me to one another in the sign language, putting their hands to their chins and then stroking down to their waists indicating their idea of my whiskers, I decided to shave.

Both the Kiowas and the Comanches were splendid horsemen. Bone-e-tah, when he sat astride his horse, rode like a centaur. He and the horse seemed one and the same animal. The Indians were very proud of their horses.

Captain Scott, the commanding officer, told a number of the Kiowas how the white men trained the fire horses in the cities. He told them that when the alarm sounded, the horses were trained to run and take their places in front of the fire engines. The Kiowas listened incredulously.

"White man heap smart," they said, "but no horse do that."

Later several of the Kiowa chiefs went on a mission to Washington, D. C. Captain Scott accompanied them. While in the national capital he arranged to take them to a fire house to see the horses in action. He told the firemen about the argument he had had with the natives.

When all of the chiefs were in the fire house, the firemen turned on a practice alarm. The horses jumped into position by the fire engine exactly as Captain Scott said they did it. It all happened so fast that the Indians were taken completely by surprise. They fell all over each other trying to keep out of the way of the horses.

In the fire house not a word was said by any of them. They left the fire house single file, Captain Scott bringing up the rear. They were silent until they reached the hotel, where Captain Scott asked them what they thought of the white man's fire engine horses.

"White man heap smart," they said. "White man's horses heap smart."

CHAPTER ELEVEN

AMONG THE PAI-UTES

One of the most misunderstood of the Indian tribes was the Ute nation, shortened from Pai-utes. They lived in southern Utah, a desert country with occasional water holes around which the Utes established their villages.

In the early days the Spanish explorers called these people "the cowardly Utes," because the natives considered wisdom the greater part of valor. When they were attacked by the warlike Navajos across the Grand Canyon, the Utes made it a practice to retire from their villages to the colorful canyons of Utah, which were natural fortresses, where they had cached food and supplies sufficient to last until the invaders returned home.

The Utes acquired a bad reputation in the early sixties when they were charged with the New Ulm Massacre. A party of men, women, and children were annihilated in southern Utah while en route to California. The Utes were supposed to have committed the outrage, although subsequent observation showed that it was inspired largely by renegade white men.

In spite of their reputation as "the cowardly Utes," these natives subsequently proved that they were great fighters when the white men moved in on their lands to stay. They were one of the hardest of the Indian tribes to conquer and one of the last to surrender to the white man's authority.

The Utes had developed an unusual system of government. Each tribe acknowledged the authority of the "Great Chief of the Utes," who traveled over the southern Utah country and acted as arbitrator of differences between the tribes. Under their plan of diplomatic relationship, members of one tribe might visit other Ute villages if they announced themselves in advance; if they slipped in unannounced, they were trespassers and the penalty might be death. Unfortunately the early white men who came into this country did not understand the law of the Utes. If they had observed it, there might have been much less bloodshed between the Utes and the early settlers.

I found the Utes among the most friendly and least superstitious of all the tribes I visited. They were always willing to pose for me and ready to help me.

The good sense of the Utes was impressed upon me soon after I began work among them. I was painting an Indian woman and her child. The mother posed with a little papoose a few months old in his cradle, sitting with the cradle leaning against her knee. Before I finished the picture, the baby took sick and died.

If that had occurred among some other tribes, I would have been in serious trouble. The superstitious natives would have accused me of bad medicine. Some of them would have taken it so seriously that I would have been lucky to escape with my life.

The Ute mother and the others of the tribe did not blame me in any way. In fact, the mother brought another baby a little older and continued to pose so that I could finish the picture.

It was fascinating to watch this Indian woman prepare her papoose for the cradle. First she tied its arms close to its body with a thong, so that the baby could not move its limbs. Then she put in the cradle several handfuls of dead leaves, which were readily removed when soiled. After this the baby was tucked in, and it was usually content to stay there all day long.

The cradle containing the baby could be carried on the mother's back, set in a corner, or suspended from an upper branch of a tree. I cannot think of a more convenient method of handling a baby, and recommend the Indian cradle to white mothers.

While I was at the Ute reservation, Roy Hall, the Indian trader, staged a Fourth of July celebration for the Indians. He went to a great deal of work to make it a good celebration and one which the Indians could enjoy. Knowing them well, he saw to it that there were plenty of events in which the Indians could compete for prizes or side bets. They included catching greased pigs, climbing greased poles, tugs of war, foot races, sack races, and horse races. He saw to it that everyone in the tribe could take part in the contest.

At the celebration a party of Mexicans appeared with a horse upon which they were prepared to bet a large sum if the Utes would race them. The Utes, likewise, had a horse which they were prepared to back to the limit. They took up a collection among themselves, raising about four hundred dollars, which they gave to the Indian trader to hold for them. In a short time the Mexicans had covered it.

The road over which the race was to be run was next selected. The Mexicans got busy smoothing and cleaning their side of the track, and the Indians did the same with their lane.

When the Mexicans brought up their horse, on which was mounted a small Mexican boy riding with saddle, bridle, and whip, I said to myself, "This horse is sure to win."

Then the Utes brought out their horse. Astride the animal was a tiny Ute boy stark naked, his hair done up on top of his head. He rode without a saddle, and for a whip he carried only a buckskin thong. After seeing the Ute entry I was not so sure the Mexicans would win.

After several false starts the horses got away. They ran neck and neck until they were within fifty feet of the end of the course. Both sides were cheering and yelling. Excitement was at a high pitch as the Indians' horse, spurred by its midget rider, nosed out to win by a head.

The Ute nation went wild and tore down to the

trader's store, shouting and singing, to collect their
bets. Dressed in their native costumes, painted and
feathered for the celebration, they came as near representing a tribe of Indians on the war path as anything I have ever seen. The Mexicans conceded the
race to be fair and, like good sports, gathered around
to congratulate the little Ute jockey.

For a time I thought that I had lost among the Utes
my Indian name, Many-Brushes. Every time I met
a Ute, he would say, "Mike."

"These Indians must think I am an Irishman," I
told the Indian trader. "They always call me Mike."

He laughed, and said, "Mike means 'hello' in Ute."

So I was still Many-Brushes.

I enjoyed my visit among the Utes so much that I
planned to return as soon as possible. However, it
was several years before I could do so. Then I found
that the Indians had learned from the neighboring
whites to build fences and bridges, good homes, and
to cultivate their fields. They had donned white men's
clothes and had become civilized. I made several
sketches of them dressed as they were, but the drawings had little interest. So far as I was concerned,
the Utes were "spoiled Indians."

CHAPTER TWELVE

THE RICH OSAGES

When I arrived among the Osages whose reservation in Oklahoma had become the center of an oil field, they were already the wealthiest of all Indian tribes. Nevertheless when I asked to paint their portraits, they replied in the old familiar vein—"How much?"

I offered them the regular fee of two dollars a day. They scorned the proposition.

"How is it that you offer to pay us money when we have money to hire white people to work for us?" one of them asked.

The Osages delighted to display their wealth. They spent their money as fast as they received it. They loved to tell a white man to go and chop wood for them, or to harness a team. They paid the poor whites twenty-five cents for such chores.

Most of them lived in fine wooden houses which were practically barren of furniture. Often there would be a cookstove and nothing else. The Indians slept and ate on the floor.

While I was on the reservation one old Osage with

a big family and plenty of money saw a fine shiny new hearse in town. Thinking this would make a fine carriage for his family, he bought it. It was a great sight to see him taking his family out for a ride—the chief sitting on the driver's seat and the squaw and the papooses in back where the coffin ordinarily was carried.

Another Osage, who suddenly became oil rich, went to town and bought a five-thousand-dollar automobile. After taking a driving lesson, he drove away in style. Next day, he limped back to the agency, footsore and bandaged. His explanation of his adventures was this:

"Drive heap big car. Buy moonshine, take big drink. Step on gas. Trees go by heap fast. Pretty soon, see big bridge coming down road. Turn out to let bridge go by. Bang. Automobile gone. By and by get new one."

Among the Osages I met a beautiful white girl whom the Indians had captured when she was but a baby. She had been initiated into the tribe and had lived with them so long that she was as much an Indian as the homeliest squaw. She liked the life and no one could persuade her to return to her race.

I needed a studio, and the only place the Osages would offer me was an old woodshed in which a pile of rubbish was stored. When I asked them if there were no better place on the reservation, an Osage chief told me that they considered the woodshed plenty good enough for a white man.

I had just about given up trying to persuade any of

these newly-rich Osages to pose for me, and was packing my things to leave when the Osage chief called on me. He was a fine-looking Indian and I was eager to add his portrait to my collection. He wanted to know if the president of the United States ever saw any of my paintings.

"I don't know," I said. "Why?"

He told me that the president of the United States had promised to build him a house. He thought that if the president happened to be looking at the portrait I painted of him, it would remind him of the house. He said that if I happened to notice the president looking at his picture, perhaps I could remind him of the house.

I told him that if he would pose for me and if I saw the president looking at his portrait, I would surely remind him of his promise to build the house. That settled the matter and he posed for one portrait.

Chief Black Coyotte, an Arapahoe, lived at Darlington, Oklahoma, where his tribe had been settled among the whites. He was a man of importance among the Indians, and had been a leader in the Ghost Dance when his people lived among the Sioux.

Black Coyotte once received eight hundred dollars in cash from the government for some service. He immediately bought a new team of horses for his carriage and hired a coachman. His family still lived in a tepee. It was an amusing sight to see Black Coyotte with his squaw and children step out of the carriage in style and crawl into the tepee, after which the carriage rolled on to the barn, where the coachman slept with the horses.

One day Black Coyotte came into my room while I was writing letters.

"Why don't you send telegrams?" he asked. "Go, heap quick."

He told me he had just sent a telegram to "McKinney," meaning President McKinley.

Several of Black Coyotte's children had died, and in accordance with the Indian custom, he underwent a four-day fast. During the fast, he had a dream in which the Great Spirit told him that if he wished to save the lives of his other children he must cut seventy pieces of flesh from his body and offer them to the sun. Black Coyotte did this and burned the pieces. When I painted his portrait, he insisted that I paint the scars with red paint, so that they would show plainer in the picture.

E A BURBANK
1939

Courtesy of Fred T. Darvill, San Francisco, California.
Buffalo Bill, 1939.

THE COWBOY ARTIST
CHARLES M. RUSSELL

Charles M. Russell, the Cowboy Artist, 1939.

Indian House. Burbank's Residence at Polacca, Arizona.

CHAPTER THIRTEEN

CHILDREN OF THE SUN

The Indians I knew were grown-up children, tender-hearted, filled with superstitions, joyfully appreciative of the wonders of nature. To these Children of the Sun each animal, each plant, each rock or wind or other object of nature was animated by a spirit which might be either beneficial or injurious to them personally according to the way it was propitiated or offended by the Indian's conduct.

To the Indians, certain forces of nature were especially potent, particularly the sun, as were also fire and water, the rain clouds, the eagle, the rattlesnake, and the buffalo. Changing conditions and the influence of the white man were rapidly undermining these simple beliefs, but they had not changed the Indian entirely. It was my good fortune to know many tribes intimately before the white man's domination had completely destroyed the customs of the real Americans.

I found the Indians poetic to a high degree. Some of their sagas were epic in their conception. Often their myths showed a fine vein of humor.

The dances which followed the feasting and the ceremonies to propitiate the gods were of great variety. It seemed to me that an Indian could make music out of anything—a drum, a reed, an eagle bone, a rattle, or even a notched stick resting on a gourd.

The Indians had songs for every occasion—lullabies, songs for work or love or games or medicine, war and ceremonials. Although some of these to my unpracticed ears were merely noises, others had great rhythm and beauty.

Among all the tribes I was impressed with the kindness and generosity displayed by the Indians toward all children. They seemed to find it easy to make life enjoyable for children since they are but grown-up children themselves.

From the time the Indian boy was born until he was married, he thought of life as full of pleasure. Usually he had few cares, doing little besides hunting, fishing, and engaging in the varied activities that most youngsters long for. The Pueblo children, however, were the exception to the rule.

Wherever I went among the Indians I found them fond of their pets, particularly the dogs. Almost always among a group of Indians I would find a wild animal which had been raised and made a pet.

One tribe had a wolf cub which they had raised. The wolf had become quite tame and I often played with him, cuffing his head from side to side. When he would growl I would put my hand in his mouth, but instead of biting it he would lick my hand. This wolf cub would lie perfectly still as though asleep until a chicken would come within reach, then quick as a flash he would nab it.

I was away for three months and upon my return the Indians told me not to go near the wolf as he was mad and would bite. He was chained up, and when I approached him he backed off the full length of the chain. I pulled him toward me, talking all the time. At last he seemed to recognize me and when I laid hands on him he played with me as usual.

At Fort Sill the Indians had a pet bear that gave them lots of fun. They would scratch his back with a stick, after which he would roll over on his back so that they could scratch his stomach. As they scratched, he would growl with delight.

At one village the Indians had tamed a mocking-bird. They had taught him to whistle a tune. He had learned all but the last note. I spent much time trying to get him to finish the tune, whistling it over and over for him. I had about given him up as too dumb to learn the tune when he whistled it clear through just to show that he could do it.

This bird loved to tease an old mother hen by making clucks just as the hen would to warn her flock that a hawk was approaching. The mocker would also cluck to call the brood for food, whereupon the chicks would come running to their mother only to be disappointed.

Often, in talking with Indians who posed for me and who did not speak English, I used the sign language. Thus to tell an Indian to pose, the motion was to hold out the left hand and with the right a few inches away make the motion of drawing. At one reservation a white man had a smart little dog named "Bow-Wow." This dog had seen me make the sign for posing so many times that one day when I made the motion to him, he ran and sat in the chair. So I made a painting of him in oil while he posed.

In spite of the white man's domination, the Indians were true children of nature. In their hearts they remained forever loyal to their first teacher. Their artistry was copied directly from the hills and plains over which they roamed. With them imitation took the place of invention. They worked not from models but from such materials as nuts, berries, bones, elk teeth, furs, skins, feathers, porcupine quills, and the like.

In their attempts at artistic reproduction, an innate taste betrays itself. One has to understand and estimate their work properly to appreciate how marvellous it is both in design and color.

If an Indian takes the trouble to explain his inspiration to you, you can readily trace in a single basket or rug different flowers or birds, various animals, the sun, moon, and stars, the marking on the backs of snakes, and other natural decorations. No matter what the pattern is, the Indian finds his designs and colors in nature and the objects surrounding him.

Once when an Indian woman was trying to explain to me the reason for putting yellow next to purple in a rug, she showed me a flower with a purple center.

"The Great Spirit made that," she said.

One would naturally think that with all the Indians looking to nature for their designs, they would have a sameness, but that is not so. In a sense the different tribes of Indians were as different as several schools of art. The work of each tribe varies materially from the art of another.

There could hardly be a greater difference as, for example, there is in the work of the Sioux as compared with that of the Hopis, yet all copy directly from nature.

Even among closely related tribes, each group has its distinctive characteristics. The Zunis and the Hopis resemble one another more nearly than the other tribes, yet the manner in which they take their designs from birds, animals, clouds, and rainbows shows many distinctive characteristics.

All Indians are essentially artistic. Although the women excel in basket making, pottery, and rugs, the artistic taste is by no means confined to them. Indian men show an equal sense of line and color in their work. In the production of bows and arrows, pipes, war bonnets, and similar articles of utility, they play an important part. Even Geronimo, although interested primarily in leading his people in war, had a fine eye for line and color.

One familiar with Indian work can easily discern to which tribe it should be credited. You cannot fail but be impressed by the fact that nature is viewed through different eyes by each tribe. Allegiance to tribal tradition seems to be regarded as a duty, and the work seems to transform the various tribes into as many different art schools.

At Ganado, Arizona, Mr. Hubbell, an Indian trader, collected patterns of the finest Navajo rugs and blankets. He had them painted in oil and water colors and urged the Navajo women to make blankets in patterns indicated by the paintings. I have watched them studying the patterns and colors and then, with their hands, measuring off the size they should be, after which a squaw would produce a blanket exactly like the picture in color and design.

The finest Indian baskets I ever saw were made by Dat-so-law-ley, a large fat squaw living at Carson City, Nevada. Some of her baskets required a year of labor in the making. She had received as high as fifteen hundred dollars for baskets no more than two feet in diameter. Some were woven in many colors, and into others she worked different colored feathers. Her work was so unusual that a book was published showing her baskets in colors.

Most Indians are expert basket makers, but there is a great difference in the quality of their work. I think, however, that this quality difference is largely due to the fact that some Indians live in regions that produce better materials than do others. Given the same quality of willows and grass, there would be little difference in the baskets made by the various tribes.

The Hopis were particularly artistic in basket making. They dyed the materials they used, producing by a skillful blending of colors various striking effects. The California Indians wove colored feathers in very graceful designs in basket work.

This branch of art afforded the Indians perhaps their best opportunity to display their taste and imagination. I have always enjoyed watching these native Americans at work at their tasks. I never ceased to marvel at how carefully they worked, especially in blending the different colors. Often it took them a long time to get the desired harmony but they kept at it until they accomplished their purpose. I have seen a squaw work for hours experimenting on a single design.

It surprised me to find so many fine artists among both the men and the women. Haw-gone, the Kiowa Indian, was a splendid artist, painting chiefly from memory. One of his pictures was reproduced in an eastern magazine.

Chief Naiche, the Apache at Ft. Sill, who painted on deer skin, did wonderfully fine work. When Millet, the great artist, was in Chicago, he saw a deer skin that I had had Naiche paint for Mr. Ayer. Millet told Mr. Ayer it was the most beautiful decorative thing he had ever seen. Mr. Ayer made him a present of it and Millet took it back to Europe with him.

A Hopi Indian made a set of water color pictures of all the gods in their gaudy costumes. There were over a hundred of them. The government had the collection reproduced in colors in book form, and the volume is to be found today in many libraries.

The Indians were also clever wood carvers and

jewelry makers. In fact, their clothes, their pipes, even their tepees, were often artistic creations.

In all their art they regularly strove for excellence, not so much to bring out individual cleverness, but to maintain tribal characteristics in patterns and colors. The Indians worked on the principle that the nation is wiser than the individual, and that custom is paramount to the whims of innovation.

Main Street, Nespelem, Washington, During a Fourth of July
Celebration.

Indian Encampment near the Colville Indian Agency during the
Fourth of July Celebration at Nespelem, Washington.

Colville Indian Agency, Nespelem, Washington.

Nespelem School Band, 1941-42.

PO-KA-GON, THE POTAWATAMI

Chief Pokagon was born in Bertrand, Michigan, in 1825. He was baptized in the name of Simon Pokagon.

At the time of his birth the Potawatami Indians still owned a large tract of land at the end of Lake Michigan, and every spring and autumn they would go there with their families and put up their wigwams at the place called "She-gong-ong" (Chicago), which had been one of the richest hunting grounds for buffalo and other game.

Although alike in many respects, the tribe was divided into two divisions. The Michigan Indians were known as the Potawatami-of-the-Woods, while those who came from Wisconsin, and had wandered much over the prairie country, were known as the Potawatami-of-the-Prairie Indians.

The former were engaged in agriculture to some extent, and were susceptible to the influence of civilization and religion. The Prairie Indians, on the other hand, despised the cultivation of the soil, and deemed the capture of the chase the only fit food for a valorous people.

The tribe used to come and go on their nomadic excursions according to their habits, and while in the Chicago vicinity lived in wigwams near the river at a point where it is now spanned by the State Street bridge.

The movements of the Indians were regarded with great interest by the traders located in the neighborhood, who were anxious to sell them supplies in exchange for the furs which the Indians brought in. In those times the traders and soldiers in the district were only too glad to maintain peaceful relations with their "savage" neighbors.

When Pokagon was quite young his father was compelled to sell the tribal land of over one million acres to the United States government at a price of three cents an acre. Chicago is now located on part of that land.

His father died when Pokagon was fourteen years old. In him the Potawatami Indians lost their best friend as well as their chief. They no longer had any one to advise them and no one to help them secure their rights. For the government had not kept its promise and had not paid them for their valuable land. Consequently they were very poor.

Pokagon was sent to school for several years, and when he returned to his people he became their chief. He realized fully the state into which his tribe was rapidly drifting, and a sincere man, he made great efforts to secure some degree of justice for them.

He made several trips to Washington to try to persuade the United States government to pay the
claims of his people for the sale of their land, but
though his claims were just, and though he had copies
of all the necessary legal documents to prove them so,
little attention was paid to his pleading. But he
persisted, and later, when Lincoln was president,
his case was reviewed and part of the money paid.

The Potawatami Indians took part in the Civil
War, and President Grant thanked Chief Pokagon
for his tribe's services. They smoked the pipe of
peace, but still the claim remained unpaid until
President Cleveland took the matter up, and in 1896
the Potawatami Indians received the money for the
sale of their land. The money was divided equally
among them.

Chief Pokagon then settled down to a quiet life
on a little farm. He was an advocate of temperance,
and wrote articles and made many fine speeches on
the subject. He was a forceful speaker. At the time
of the World's Fair in Chicago, Mayor Harrison, Sr.,
invited Pokagon to attend the fair as a guest of the
city. He went, and delivered a very fine speech on
that occasion.

When I went to paint his portrait, I drove over to
his farm where I found him planting seed in the old
way by walking and casting the seed on the ground.
I told him of my errand, that I wished to paint his
portrait. He asked how much I would pay him, and
when I told him two dollars for six hours' sitting,
with rest period, he refused, saying that when he

worked for the government he was paid three dollars a day. He got the amount he wanted.

I told him I wanted to paint him in his Indian clothes. He said he had no Indian clothes. So I painted him as he was dressed when I met him, in his working clothes.

When it was time for him to rest he would go outdoors and read. I asked him what he was reading. He replied, "Latin." He had studied to be a priest and could read both Latin and Greek. At other times when he was resting he would be talking to some bird. He would say, "Good morning, little bird. I understand what you are saying. You are saying, 'Good morning, Pokagon.' So I say good morning to you."

He made me a present of a little book printed on birch bark and entitled, "The Plea of the Red Man." It was beautifully written. He also gave me a copy of an article an temperance, which he had written. In the article he wrote, "I cannot understand a people who can build a boat that will cross the ocean in safety and comfort, and yet cannot stop this liquor traffic."

I also met Chief Pokagon's wife, a fine old lady. She made Indian baskets, some of which I bought. Their son, Charlie, whose acquaintance I made, lived with them. I stopped with a farmer close to their home.

Pokagon told me so much about his life and about his father and the Potawatami Indians that I told him it was his duty to write a book on his life. He replied that it would be a big job.

When I had finished his portrait and was ready to leave, I hired him to take me back to the town where I was to take passage on the boat to Chicago. As we arrived in the town (I think New Haven), I prevailed upon him to go in a store and buy the paper on which to write the story. He did so, and also promised to come and see me in Chicago. But within a few days after I had finished his portrait and bade him good-by, he passed away. He died in January, 1898. He had begun his life story and his son, Charlie, finished it after his death.

APPENDIX

APPENDIX C

APPENDIX

In 1898 Pokagon's last portrait was painted, at the request of the Field Museum, by E. A. Burbank. It shows us the old chief's face weakened by age, but full of character, radiant with interest, direct and noble in its gaze, gentle and friendly in its general expression. The artist tells that these were the notable qualities in Pokagon's character, that he was a very interesting sitter to talk to, and able to speak a beautiful English. Sometimes he would be heard talking to the birds near his home. He claimed that his bird friends came every day and talked to him—perhaps he had learned their language from Lonidaw. Sometimes he talked about his Indian people, and sometimes about the large tract of land near the Chicago River that had been set aside by the government for his band, but had never been given them or paid for. The importance of articles that he had written was now recognized, and Mr. Burbank urged him to give himself no peace until he had finished his writing. Unfortunately, much of his material and all of his precious documents from his father's time were destroyed in a fire that burned his house.

The one good thing that grew out of that misfortune was that it offered an opportunity for friends to do him the kindness of building him a house as a gift. His good friend, J. C. Engle, of Hartford, Michigan, who helped him with legal advice for forty years without accepting payment, helped him now in this, and also in the still greater project of publishing the story he had written, "O-gi-maw-Kwe Mit-i-gwa-ki, Queen of the Woods," which shows his ideals, if not always the exact facts of his life. In this beautiful Indian idyl, he left us a revelation of the depths of the Indian heart. Just before it had issued from the press, the old chief died, after a very short illness, on January 27, 1898. The true friendship and the appreciation that he had met with from some of the white men must have done much to heal the wound of the injustice done by others of his tribe. An attempt was made to have his body taken to Chicago and interred with public honor in Graceland Cemetery near the grave of John Kinzie, the first white resident. Perhaps it is most fit that his quiet grave should lie, as it does, far from the great city, amid the fields of the retreat in Michigan, near the sand-dunes of South Haven and the shores of Lake Sag-i-a-gan.

Server, the narrator of the Custer Battle, told me the ground after the Custer fight was strewn with Indian clothes, war bonnets, and so forth; that the Indians in fleeing had left all the skin tepees. He said he picked up a fine Sioux Indian jacket and presented it to the Smithsonian Institute in Washington, D. C. General Terry had telegraphed to Washington, he said, asking what he should do with all the Indian clothes. The word came back, "Burn them."

When I was at the Crow Agency, Mr. and Mrs. Seton Thompson came there to see the Crow Indian war dance. Mrs. Thompson was then taking notes for an illustrated book she wrote later, entitled, *A Woman Tenderfoot Among the Rockies*—a very interesting book.

The Indians told me where some Crow Indians were buried in the tops of trees. Mr. and Mrs. Thompson and I went there. One of the bodies, that of an aged Crow Indian woman, had fallen from a tree and was lying on the ground. The Indians buried in the trees we noticed were tied there securely with leather thongs.

The three of us were standing on the hill near the trees where the Indians were buried, when two Crow Indians rode up on horseback and asked us what we were doing. I told them we wanted to see the Indians buried in trees. They said as they rode away, "No touch 'em."

I was anxious for the Thompsons to meet White Swan, and as he lived a few miles from the Crow Agency, on the other side of the Little Big Horn River, I hired a team of horses and a wagon and we drove out to meet White Swan. He was glad to see us. In his tepee he lighted his pipe of peace, took a puff himself, then passed it on to Mrs. Thompson. She took a puff, and Mr. Thompson and I did likewise. Mr. Thompson had White Swan make a set of pictures in colors for him, showing the part he took in the Custer fight.

While I was at the Crow Agency, the agent, Lieutenant Watson, showed me a letter he had just received from his good friend Remington, the artist. He said he was coming to the Crow Agency soon to fight bears, and that he wanted his scout Sharp Nose there to go with him. If he shot a bear, he wrote, he would be like the drawing he enclosed, showing him on a pedestal with his arms folded. But if he did not shoot the bear, he would be like the drawing showing the bear chasing him. Later the Santa Fe Railroad named a town after Remington, and the next town, Burbank, after me. Years afterward the agent for Burbank wrote me that it was a flourishing little town and that several Indians lived there.

Sharp Nose was at the Crow Agency when I was there waiting for Remington to come. So he posed for a picture for me, and Mr. Thompson also painted his portrait, but each of us had to pay Sharp Nose two dollars a day for posing. Unfortunately I left the Crow Agency before Remington arrived.

Mr. Mulvaney, a painter of Western subjects, painted the Custer Battle. A well known brewery in Milwaukee purchased the painting and had large lithographs made from it. They sent one to me, which I gave to a friend who has a cafe at Moss Beach, California. They are to be seen in different drinking places in California.

The Hopi Indians have their own religion, which is sacred to them. In the last few years the Baptist Church has had a missionary there, built a fine, comfortable stone church, and has made many converts. The Hopis call the Baptist converts, "Jesus people."

The Hopi converts came to church every Sunday and were there all day long. They brought their lunch with them, but the lady missionary furnished the coffee. The missionary did not want the Hopis to take part in any of the Hopi ceremonies, but some of them did on the sly.

The Hopi Indian men loved to smoke cigarettes. The missionary forbade them to smoke, but when they came to pose for me for a picture, they did want to smoke. I told them there was nothing in the Bible that read, "Thou shalt not smoke." So most of the men smoked without her knowing it.

When I was there the Hopis did not drink any whiskey. They claimed it made a man crazy. And as far as I know, they still abstain from any intoxicating drink.

The missionary had a fine organ that they would turn with a handle. Some Hopis would carry this organ up on the mesa, and the missionary and the converted Hopis would all sing sacred music, while the organ furnished the accompaniment.

They had a large tank made and filled it with water, and there they baptized the Hopis who were converted. When I was there the tank was out-of-doors, close to the church.

The missionaries didn't seem to like the artists who went to the Hopi country to paint. One of them, a lady missionary, told me it was like putting a red flag before a bull, to have any of the artists there.

The artists who went to the Hopi Indians to paint made them very happy. They paid the Hopis five dollars a month rent for the houses in the valley, just below the mesa, bought chickens and eggs from them, hired them to do their washing, paid them well for posing for pictures, paid them for running on errands miles away, and patronized the Hopi stores. And at last accounts the artists, bull or no bull, still went there to paint the Hopis and the beautiful scenery.

THE HOPI INDIAN WEDDING CEREMONY

After the *Ne-man-kochinea* there is what they call *"O-beck-ne-ah,"* where young boys and girls take their *So-me-pe-ka* and go for a picnic out beyond the mesa. There is where the lovemaking takes place. They usually select the one they want, more for riches or industry than for love. After that the girl tells her mother that she wants a certain lad; if agreeable to the mother, they grind a lot of meal, make a stack of *peki* (bread), and invite his relatives in. They all give advice on what a good husband should be, admonishing him to raise plenty of corn, get plenty of wood, and so on. Then the groom-to-be takes meat over to the girl's home and it is accepted with many thanks. At this point more advice is given and more food is served. They visit back and forth, taking presents of *peki* and meat until time for the wedding ceremony, which takes place usually after most of the winter ceremonies are over. Meantime the girl, her mother, and all of their clan women grind bushels of corn into meal that is just as fine as our flour, until they think they have more than the amount that was prepared for the last wedding. Then the groom's mother is notified that on a certain night they will bring the promised bride. The girl begins to grind and keeps grinding for three days and nights. On the second day of grinding there is a battle of mud slinging between boys and girls, relatives of the couple. This is all in fun, of course. On the third day the hair is dressed. A new pottery bowl is set in a circle of sand, the soap weed and fresh water are made into suds, and the boy's mother washes the bride's hair which is then fashioned into beautiful whirls like a married woman's. The bride's mother then washes the groom's head.

As for the men, while the women are busy making *peki*, they usually kill ten or more sheep. They card and spin cotton until they have enough for two dresses and a long belt. They make two large white blankets, and a smaller

one with dark red and blue borders, a white belt with long
streamers, and moccasins of deerskin. If they are especially
happy over the wedding, they also make a dark woven dress
for everyday wear. The girl and her relatives bring meal
often to the cave where the men are working, almost a
wagonful of meal at a time.

When all is finished the bride is bathed and dressed in the
large white blanket belted down. At sunrise the mother-in-
law takes her back to her own home, and the groom comes
when it is time to eat.

Each woman guest is supposed to bring a plaque of corn
and meal with which to make pudding called *"Pee-gum-eh,"*
which is baked overnight in the ground. Then there is another big meal.

Only once do they wear their white dress after they come
home, and that is at the *Ne-mon-Kachinea,* and then the
large white blanket is laid away for her burial robe. So you
see it takes almost a year to really get married Hopi way.

February 10, 1940

DEAR ROYCE:

I enclose something I have written about the Hopi Indians. If you wish you might add it to the manuscript.

When Miss Abbott came here to see me a few weeks ago,
she advised me not to go to see the Hopi Indians. Such a
change had taken place in them, a different people from
what they were forty years ago. Their homes modernized,
radios, automobiles, and some of them going places in air
machines. One of them had a large up-to-date store. Fine
highways to the different mesas, like all over California,
all dressed in modern civilian clothes. And all speaking
good English. And but very few of the old Indians living,
and those now living were babies when I was there.

Some of the young Indian men are splendid artists. I
saw out at Civic Center in a large gallery examples of their
work, which surprised me, in execution, all in colors, and
such fine drawing. All these pictures were to go to Treasure
Island for exhibition. Many artists would be proud if they

could do such fine work. When I was with the Hopi Indians I met several Hopi artists, and they showed me their work, which was very crude, in comparison to what I saw here.

The Hopis that made pottery then—the artistic work on all their pottery could not be better—which is true in the blankets they wove, and all their masks, and ceremonial clothes, jewelry, and so forth. How they improved as they did I do not know.

When I was at Ft. Sill, Haw-gone, a Kiowa Indian, and Naiche, an Apache, did fine artistic work. They would watch me all day long when I was painting, and I explained to them, gave them lessons, and when I arrived in Chicago, I sent both a full set of colors and the next time I went to Ft. Sill, I noticed a great improvement in their artistic work. But I think none of the Indians would be able to paint a portrait of any person that you could recognize.

Of all the Indians I knew Naiche was by far the best artist. He also was an expert wood carver. He made me a present of a cane he carved from wood, beautifully executed, then as finely painted. He had only crude tools with which to work.

November 19, 1939

DEAR ROYCE:

Miss Abbott, a dear friend of mine, has been with the Hopi Indians over forty years. She was with them when I arrived at Polacca in 1898. She retired a few years ago, as her health was not good. Miss Abbott spoke the Hopi language fluently, and knows as much about them as they do. They never had a better friend. You will notice in the manuscript, I mention very little about the Hopi marriage ceremonies. She knows all about it. I have requested that she describe it, and this should be included in the book.

She came to San Francisco a few days ago, and came to see me. I had not seen her for thirty years. She has seen all their ceremonies, and as soon as I hear from her I will let you know.

SUNLIGHT MISSION POLACCA
AND
SUNLIGHT MISSION TOREVA

In about the year nineteen hundred, while Miss Crawford was still doing mission work with the Kiowa Indians, some of the Kiowa Christians wanted to send the gospel to a tribe that did not have missionaries and accordingly sent some money to the Women's Baptist Home Mission Society, asking that a new mission be opened. Miss Mary G. Burdette, who was the corresponding secretary, made a trip out to Arizona; she went a long distance by buckboard with an Indian driver who did not know the English language; when she was hungry she said "coffee" and then they stopped to eat.

After a long, tiresome journey they came to Toreva, (Whirling water), there the National Indian Association had started a work, and were desirous of turning it over to some denomination. The mission was nearly two miles from the place of the whirling water, where Uncle Sam had a little day school. Miss Burdette reached the place at a time when the sun was pouring down its brightest rays. She thought of "The Son of righteousness with healing in His wings," and she took over that work and called it Sunlight Mission.

There had been no conversions from the six years of work that had been done by the National Indian Association. The darkness was very great and added to their condition spiritually. They had been passing through five years of drouth and the Hopi people were hungry. The name Hopi means peaceable; this they called themselves, but their enemies called them Moki which is a Hopi word also, and means dead. However, they were known for many years by that name by the Department of the Interior until someone urged they be called by their right name, Hopi, which they deserved, for they were a peaceable people.

It was in November, 1901, that Miss Mary McLean was sent from the work among the Kiowa Indians, in Oklahoma, to take up the work at Toreva, Arizona. Six miles by horseback trail was another group of three villages with about the same population as the three villages near the whirling water, and the government field matron, Miss Sarah E. Abbott, urged Miss Burdette to send workers to that place, known as Polacca. It was a little more than a year after Miss McLean went to Toreva that Miss Ida M. Schofield was sent from the Comanche Indians and Miss Abigail E. Johnson was sent from the Cheyenne Indians (of Oklahoma) to start the work at Polacca, Arizona. They arrived the day before Christmas, 1902.

At Toreva Miss McLean found a number who had been to school a short time, but no one seemed to want the job as interpreter. Finally one who had been to school only two years said he would try to tell the Hopi people what she wished to say to them. His name was Steve Quonestewa. She helped him to remember what he had learned in school, and took him on further, especially in Bible reading, and he has remained in the work until the present, 1939. Steve became a Christian during that first year's work and then there followed a stormy time of persecution for him.

When they saw that Steve believed, they told him that they would take his children away from him, but when that did not turn him back they told him they would take his wife away from him. But Steve said, "Even if should take my wife and children away from me I will follow Jesus anyway." They replied, "You will have no rain on your field if you follow Jesus," but that did not move Steve; one morning he came to the mission, his eyes just shining. Miss McLean asked, "Well, how is it this morning?" Steve replied, "It rained on my field last night." "Did it not rain on other fields?" she asked. "No, it only rained on my field." Then she said, "Did it not rain out around your field?" Again he replied, "It only rained on my field." That gave him great encouragement.

Miss Marrietta Reside had come to Toreva, was giving her services and paying her expenses, to do what she could to help the work along. It was while she was there that the lame man, another who, like Steve, had accepted Christ, and was suffering persecutions, came to the mission crying, his shirt torn into shreds. He was riding on a burro for he could not walk any distance. The missionaries inquired what had happened, and he told them that the Hopi men, who did not love Jesus, caught him and did that to him because he is a Christian. Miss Reside went to the quilt supplies and found calico and made him a shirt.

Often the chief men would bring an interpreter and come to the mission, sometimes ten, and at other times as many as fifteen men would come at one time to scold Miss McLean and order her away. She always baked lots of bread and had it on hand and when they came she made coffee and gave them some food. Then she gave them the gospel, and they went away baffeled.

She taught the Hopi women to keep their homes, their children, and their villages clean, but most of all she taught them of their need of the Savior and a clean heart.

Water was scarce at the mission station, and so the missionary got a number of Hopi men to come and help dig a well. The place that was chosen was very sandy, and after they had gone down a number of feet, while one man was still down in the dry well, one side of it caved in and the man was buried. She urged the men to go down and get him out, but as no one hurried to do so, she grabbed a shovel and jumped down into the well and began to work to save his life. Soon then the men followed her example, and the man was rescued.

Sometimes white people who came into Hopiland would laugh and say, "You will not get water enough to baptize these people by immersion. They will have to be sprinkled." But a short while before time to baptize the converts, a little spring which was just over the line of the mission property, on the Hopi land, closed up and then burst out on the mission property. Miss McLean had the spring cleaned out and walled up and the first converts were baptized in the spring.

When Miss Burdette took over the work at Toreva from

the National Indian Association, there were two small frame buildings there. One was the house in which the missionaries lived, the other was a little building which was used as a laundry. Miss McLean had the Hopi women come there to wash their clothes, getting the water from an old spring which had been walled up by the old Catholic Fathers in the sixteenth century.

In that first year that the work was started by the Baptists, an addition was built to the house. It was of stone, and made the work much easier, as the larger room of the frame building was then used for services. The mission had a bell which was perched high on an iron frame and could be heard from the villages upon the mesa. It became a custom to ring the bell at sunrise Sunday mornings, so that no one could say he or she did not know that it was Sunday, and so did not come.

Five years after the work started the missionary got a number of Hopi men to help her put up a church building. That was in 1906, and they are using the same building yet. The money for the work of building was provided by the Women's American Baptist Home Mission Society. Then with some money given to her to use as she wished (as her cousin expressed it) she built a long, low building which she planned to use as a hospital. However, that plan was not fully carried out by the mission for the government had plans for a hospital, although it was not built until several years later.

In 1929 the community house was built, and repairs were made on the mission house and a Delco plant installed. For fourteen years (since 1925) the mission has been provided with a car; as in the early years the missionaries went horseback and for a few years they had a buggy and used two horses.

The church was organized in 1907 and has grown until it now numbers between forty and fifty, and many have gone home to be with the Lord. Of that number is the lame man who suffered persecution as recorded above, and Pliny, who was horsewhipped when he became a Christian and who, in later years, became our evangelist and for several years did faithful service for the Lord.

In the fall of 1914 the mission house and little laundry building burned down. Then again the W. A. B. H. M. Society sent the money and the present building was erected. Rev. Lee I. Thayer, who was then at Keam Canyon, superintended the work. He was pastor of the two Hopi churches at that time.

Aside from the regular Sunday school, church services, and prayer meetings, the mission conducts two sewing meetings for women, one for men in the winter months, and one for children Saturdays during the months when school is in session. There are also many other things of interest, such as stereoptican lectures, and so forth.

Miss McLean remained in the work at Toreva for ten years, then resigned. Mrs. Bertha Beeman and Miss Anna Nelson carried on the work for a number of years. Mrs. Beeman married Mr. J. H. Kirkland, and Miss Nelson married and lives in the East. Then followed a succession of workers. The present workers are Miss Lolita J. Stickler and Miss Mable Olsen.

In answer to the prayers of Miss Sarah E. Abbott, a deaconess, who was the government field matron at Polacca, missionaries were sent to that place a year after Miss McLean had taken up the work at Toreva.

There was a long, low, flat-roof building belonging to the government, which opened into the court opposite the building Miss Abbott occupied. It had not been used for three years. For a number of days she worked to prepare that building for the missionaries.

Shortly before the arrival of Miss Schofield and Miss Johnson, there was a fall of snow which broke the long dry spell, and the Hopi people gave those new workers the credit for that good change in the weather. "Surely they must have good hearts." This was the opinion of many of the Hopi men and women.

The government agent, Mr. Burton, at Keams Canyon, allowed the day school at Polacca to be used for services

Sundays, and gave the missionaries permission to have chapel exercises with the school children each day. One teacher at Polacca had the children come down Sunday mornings to bathe, then to sit in their seats and sing and listen to a Bible lesson. This went on for nearly a year. Many of the fathers and mothers stood listening while the message was given to the children, then after they were dismissed, these older ones sat in the seats and listened to a message which was interpreted.

George Lomayesva and his wife, who had been in school four years at Keams Canyon, interpreted the word. The wife, Myra, took a strong stand for the Lord and was baptized before George was. She was a faithful interpreter for thirty-four years, then she went to her heavenly home.

Large numbers came to the services until they found that God's word was against idol worship and any other except the worship of the Lord Jesus, the Son of God, then many of them stayed away; and every Sunday morning men were stationed at the head of the trails leading to the meeting place and told the people to go back home and not listen to the teaching any more.

For a number of months the missionaries baked bread and cooked beans and served lunch, to those who desired to go home with them and sing the songs they learned in the boarding school in Keams Canyon; for there they had used Gospel hymns 1-6. The hymns were explained and interpreted to those who did not understand English. Many rich gospel messages were brought out and sung into the hearts of the Hopi people.

Because attendance at meetings still grew less, the missionaries went once a week to the villages, holding a meeting in a home in one village in the afternoon and after eating their lunch in Hongovi's home, in the middle village, they would hold a service in his home at night. But when only those who came to the regular services would be present at such meetings, they changed their plans. They went from house to house holding services in each home. Sometimes they would have as many as seven services in one afternoon.

George and Myra were living in the middle village yet, and she always went along to interpret. A young man who was a believer, Letseoma by name, went along to help in singing. Occasionally he used a zobo horn; he would also lead in prayer. A guitar was used in those little meetings. We knew the people were enjoying them, but finally we realized there had been more opposition, for the family would go out of the house always leaving a deaf person with us. So the little house-to-house meetings were abandoned.

Later an old man took Letseoma and threatened to kill him if he did not stop going down to the schoolhouse to listen to the Jesus Road. A slight earthquake had caused a place on one side of the mesa to sink down, and rocks to roll down, injuring a peach orchard. The old men blamed Letseoma for this. They said to him, "You have been out there sprinkling meal and praying for that to take place," but he replied, "I do not pray that way with meal any more, and I have not prayed to have the mesa fall, when I pray I talk to God in the name of Jesus." They answered, "But if you will not stop going to Sunday school we will put you in a dark room, and if you will not promise to stop we will kill you."

Letseoma replied, "I will not stop listening to Jesus' word. He has saved me and He will save you, too, if you will believe Him." Just then a young man came along and although not a believer, he persuaded them to let Letseoma go.

When the Hopi people have their ceremonies everyone in the village has to help in some way. Women have to cook for the dancers, and the men furnish extra flour and meat. Thus the believers saw that the only way to be out-and-out for the Lord, they would have to move away from the villages and build homes. This they proceeded to do.

Some land at Polacca, chosen by Miss McLean, had been set aside for mission purposes. As yet there were no buildings belonging to the mission. White people who saw that the government buildings could not be used permanently, gave money so that a small building could be put up. Miss Abbott gave thirty dollars, which was used to buy windows, a door, and some lumber that could be used for the ceiling and window frames. Because the Hopi people had very little corn, due to the drouth, Mrs. Gates asked the Kansas farmers to donate corn to the Hopi Indians. The Indians were to work for the corn. It was given to the missionaries and they and the Hopi men came and cut out rock for a small building. There were two lady artists on the reservation, and at that time they were leaving to go to another place, and they gave their tents to the missionaries. One of the tents was used to buy logs for the room. The plan was to make a Hopi roof. It would be flat, and so logs were used to hold the brush and clay, and the ceiling lumber.

Mr. Collins, who had been a government agent in Keams Canyon years before, was out on the reservation doing some work with a bunch of Hopi men. There were a few hours left when the work was completed and he took his men over to the little mission house and let them finish out the day by putting on the roof. By cooking and having working parties (the people work for their dinner) the building was finished, the mud mixed and plastered on the roof, the floor plastered and polished, and the house was ready for use.

There had been a great deal of opposition to the "Jesus Road," and fewer people came to services. It was thought best not to have meetings in the government school building any longer, so those who still were brave enough to come met in the little mission house. The Sunday dinners also were discontinued, and the people brought their lunches, the missionaries furnishing coffee and sugar. Soon after moving into the mission house for services the song services turned into a prayer meeting for those who wished to follow the Lord. At Toreva Mission Miss McLean had started that method of work, and it was thought best to follow her example. What a joy that was to see them come, one or two at a time, to join the prayer group, fully determined to leave all to follow Him at any cost.

In 1910 Rev. Lee I. Thayer came to Keams Canyon to do missionary work among the Navajos and to become pastor of the two Hopi churches. The Christians had been bap-

tized by Mr. Young and Mr. McCourtney. Mr. Young baptized the first six, and organized the church at Toreva in 1907. Miss McLean and Miss Johnson both joined by letter (Miss Schofield had gone to the MoMo Indians before that time). The next year Mr. McCourtney baptized a number of believers, and organized the church at Polacca. These men were doing the work of evangelism in Arizona.

As soon as Mr. Thayer came to the work at Keams Canyon, he not only had to erect buildings for that mission, but he had charge of the building at Polacca. The Women's A. B. H. M. Society appropriated money for a good church building, and in June, 1910, it was dedicated. In 1920 the community house was built, which was fitted up for a laundry. It was thought that to get into touch with the women during wash days would further the work of giving the gospel. After trying out that method it was deemed best to let the women go to the day school laundry, and the building was made over into a community house, where the women come to sew and hear the gospel, and where programs are held at Christmas time. The house for missionaries was also made over and added to until it would take pages to tell the changes that were made, and of the water supply for both missions; also of the lighting plant that was installed at Polacca, and of the Mission car.

Over west from our Baptist missions the Mennonites have also established missions among the Hopi people. With them we have worked in harmony. They made translations of some of the scriptures, and gave copies to both missions, which were used in teaching the believers and also in visits to the villages.

Christmas is a time when crowds of Hopi people come to the mission, and the gospel has the greatest place on the program. The Christian men tell them that Christ took our place on Calvary's Cross that we might have eternal life with Him. It is a time when the Christians urge the people to accept the Gift of God.